HBR Guide to
Office Politics

Harvard Business Review Guides

Arm yourself with the advice you need to succeed on the job from the most trusted brand in business. Packed with how-to essentials from leading experts, the HBR Guides provide smart answers to your most pressing work challenges.

The titles include:

HBR Guide to Better Business Writing

HBR Guide to Finance Basics for Managers

HBR Guide to Getting the Mentoring You Need

HBR Guide to Getting the Right Job

HBR Guide to Getting the Right Work Done

HBR Guide to Giving Effective Feedback

HBR Guide to Making Every Meeting Matter

HBR Guide to Managing Stress

HBR Guide to Managing Up and Across

HBR Guide to Persuasive Presentations

HBR Guide to Project Management

HBR Guide to
Office Politics

Karen Dillon

Copyright 2013 Harvard Business School Publishing Corporation

All rights reserved

Printed in the United States of America

What You'll Learn

Every organization has its share of political drama: Personalities clash. Agendas compete. Turf wars erupt. It can make you crazy if you're trying to keep your head down and get your job done.

The problem is, you can't just keep your head down. You need to work productively with your colleagues—even the challenging ones—for the good of your organization and your career.

How can you do that without crossing over to the dark side? By acknowledging that power dynamics and unwritten rules exist—and by constructively navigating them. "Politics" needn't be a dirty word. You can succeed at work without being a power grabber or a corporate climber, and the expert advice in this guide will help.

You'll get better at:

- Building relationships with difficult people

- Gaining allies and influencing others

- Wrangling the resources you need

What You'll Learn

- Moving up without ruffling feathers

- Dealing with the boss's pet

- Coping with office bullies and cliques

- Claiming credit when it's due

- Avoiding power games and petty rivalries

- Collaborating with competitive peers

Contents

Contents

Section 2: POLITICAL CHALLENGES WITH YOUR COLLEAGUES

Section 3: POLITICAL CHALLENGES IN YOUR ORGANIZATION

Introduction

Every office is political.

For years, I naively thought I worked at a place that wasn't. I saw our office as more or less fair, more or less healthy, and highly inclusive—perhaps overly so—in decision making. People competed with *themselves*, I'd proudly tell prospective recruits, not with one another. And I meant it.

All those good things I believed? They were true—but only to a point, I realize with hindsight. We competed with ourselves, but also with one another. Our bosses had favorites, and we noticed. We grumbled about promotions that didn't seem deserved, assignments that didn't seem fair. People subtly found ways to elbow one another out of pole position for C-suite attention. Our office was political. Of course it was.

In a 2011 survey by the UK-based management-consulting firm Revelation, 95% of respondents said that manipulation and hidden agendas in the workplace had affected them personally. So you're in good company if these issues make you crazy. Maybe you're plagued by an office bully who constantly questions what you're doing and undermines you in meetings. Or a boss who pits you against your peers. Or a clique that wields an inordinate amount of organizational power. Perhaps you've even encountered backstabbing, one-upmanship, or shifting alliances.

You can't escape politics—no matter what your role or function. That's what Franke James, founder of OfficePolitics.com, has learned from the professionals around the world sharing their struggles on her website. It's inevitable even if you're self-employed. "If you're dealing with clients," James says, "you're dealing with their office politics, too. You have to make them look good. You have to understand the dynamics behind the scenes for them."

Does that mean you have to fight fire with fire? Connive and scheme? Get your blows in faster? No. As the experts and consultants cited in this guide argue, you can weather—and even participate in—politics without selling your soul. They base this observation on research, their work with clients, and abundant personal experience. And it's supported by the many examples (real but disguised) I've included throughout.

So what's the solution? It's about being *constructively* political—understanding personal dynamics among colleagues, working together for mutual advantage, and ultimately focusing on the good of the enterprise.

What happens if you simply do what's asked of you and mutter about colleagues who curry favor? Executive coach Beth Weissenberger, cofounder of the Handel Group, says you're doing yourself in. She's seen it happen again and again in her years of coaching: Those who try to stay completely out of the political fray are less likely to meet their job and career goals than those who engage.

So she advises her clients to stop getting worked up about the unfairness of it all and build their own positive relationships with colleagues who will help them do their jobs well.

Ron Ashkenas, a managing partner at Schaffer Consulting, agrees. As he puts it: "It's easy to use politics as an excuse for a lack of achievement or an outlet for your frustration. But it's a lot more effective to use politics as a way to get things done." This guide will help you do that. Here are some common themes you'll notice throughout:

- **Question your reaction:** When people appear to be playing political games, we often think we know their motives, but sometimes we're off the mark. Step back and reevaluate: What else could be driving the behavior? Maybe it's not as vengeful as it seems—or even intentional.

- **Try removing yourself from the equation:** Everybody brings her own quirks, worries, and stresses to work. What you assume is a personal attack may have absolutely nothing to do with you.

- **Take charge of your fate:** Even if the playing field isn't level, you'll accomplish little by complaining about it. Assume responsibility for your progress. Don't give your manager and others any reason to dismiss you as a whiner.

- **Keep your cool:** Office bullies and other game players win every time they see they've rattled you. Never give them that satisfaction—you'll just perpetuate the problem. Stay composed, and they'll lose their power.

When asked to write this guide, I jumped at the chance. Since I understood the challenges people faced, I'd approach it with empathy. But secretly, I also felt a little smug—I thought I'd successfully navigated most political scenarios in my career. Then, after interviewing about 20 experts and synthesizing their advice on the various dilemmas, I recognized several mistakes I'd made over the years: stewing over injustices, fighting the wrong battles, making things personal when they didn't need to be. Now, looking back at those moments, I wish I'd done my research sooner.

It's never too late to learn, though—thank goodness for that.

So what's the main takeaway, if I had to boil it down to one? As organizational development and HR expert Susan Heathfield puts it, don't try to be the boss's pet—be *everyone's* pet. That is, devote your energy to being a terrific employee and colleague. You'll find that you're less preoccupied with all the jockeying that's going on around you—and more focused on positive pursuits like performance, growth, and fulfillment.

Section 1
Political Challenges with Your Boss

Chapter 1
The Boss Who Holds You Back

The Problem

You've been quietly showing your boss the ropes for a long time. He relies on you heavily for help with everything from interpreting monthly reports to sizing up market demand to placating cranky stakeholders. Yet only his name appears on the e-mails that update higher-ups on your projects. You feel like the stagehand behind the curtain—you're running the show, but he's the one out front, taking a prolonged bow.

Why It Happens

When the person who should be your organizational guide and cheerleader keeps your smart contributions under wraps, of course you don't feel valued. Even if he's not intentionally undermining you or holding you back, it's hard to stay motivated—after all, you know your efforts will go unrecognized.

Some bosses simply don't like sharing the spotlight. Others get nervous when their shortcomings are thrown into sharp relief by a direct report's strengths. You may run into this problem with a boss who is new to his job, for example, and feels threatened by your deep organizational knowledge and close internal ties. Or perhaps your manager inherited you in a merger or a reorg and has discovered that you bring critical new skills to his team—skills everyone assumed he already had.

What to Do About It

You may fantasize about changing jobs, but you probably won't have to resort to that. You can improve your day-to-day relationship with your manager—but you'll need to lead the transformation.

Own the problem

Jessica Pryce-Jones, CEO of the UK-based leadership consultancy iOpener and author of *Happiness at Work*, says people are often too quick to dub a work relationship a failure before taking their share of responsibility for fixing it.

How can you do your part? Remember that your boss wants to succeed in his job as much as you do in yours. That will help you adopt a constructive mind-set so that you can move beyond your frustration and improve the dynamic. Think about what you share with your boss rather than what divides you: If you have only "transactional" conversations, Pryce-Jones says, you're unlikely to warm to each other. But looking for personal similarities will make it easier for you to connect professionally. Did you grow up in the same area? Do you admire the same people?

BRANCHING OUT: ALEXY'S STORY

WHAT HAPPENED:

I had a "dive-bomb" manager. He'd disappear for weeks with very little contact, until he got wind of some project I was involved in. Then he would swoop in and demand reports, details, every scrap of information he could get. These urgent requests came in the form of rat-a-tat e-mails arriving at 10 PM or later. Often he'd take my responses to board meetings, passing the work off as his own. Then he'd lecture me on the need to keep him in the loop.

WHAT I DID:

I tried to keep my boss informed, but he'd ignore my updates and still somehow be taken by surprise. So I found myself pointing him to e-mails or memos I'd sent weeks earlier, which just annoyed him. I started to feel cut off from the rest of the organization, so I reached out to managers above him, asking if I could help with their cross-functional initiatives. That way, when he came back and demanded to know what was going on, I could say, "So-and-so signed off," and he'd have to drop it. I also began to let people know what ideas and contributions were mine because he was taking credit for everything. I copied key people on my e-mail updates to him, spoke up more in meetings, made casual comments that showed my depth of knowledge, and attached my name to documents I created for him.

DID ALEXY GET IT RIGHT?

It's hard to strike a healthy balance with an alternately indifferent and needy boss who shuts you off from others. Alexy was smart to put his name on his contributions and form alliances with other senior managers—otherwise, he'd have remained isolated and resentful—but it probably wasn't the best idea to go behind his paranoid boss's back (or above his head). That just fed the perception that he couldn't be trusted with independence and visibility.

Finding common ground will help you interpret events and interactions more positively. Are there reasonable explanations for what you perceive as negative signals? Maybe your boss appears to be shutting you out of critical meetings with his boss, for instance—but it's really because one-on-ones feel more efficient to him, not because he wants to keep you from growing and advancing.

Once you're open to his point of view, you can begin treating him as you'd like to be treated: Find genuine opportunities to make him look good. "Tell someone he respects—perhaps one of his peers—about an insight he shared with you or something he accomplished that you admired," Pryce-Jones suggests. And express your appreciation after he helps you meet an important goal or solve a tough problem. You don't need to be effusive. Just sincerely acknowledge what he's done for you. At the very least, you'll lower his defenses. Best case, you'll set a gracious example that he wants to follow.

Tap his former direct reports

If you can easily get in touch with someone who used to work for your boss, invite her out for coffee. (You may already know someone who managed the relationship effectively if you've been in the organization for a while. Otherwise, you might need to rely on friends to discreetly point you in the right direction.) Explain that you're eager to develop in your role and that you'd like to pick her brain about her experience working with and learning from your boss. Pitch it as a tutorial for you, not as a gripe session: See if she can share insights about his mentoring style, for example, and tips on how to earn his trust so that he'll feel comfortable giving you stretch assignments and placing you on cross-functional teams. Even if you feel safe confiding in this person, assume that anything you say could make its way back to your boss and edit yourself accordingly.

If the former report has only bad news for you—your boss really *is* a jerk—at least you're forewarned. You know it's not personal to you and that someone else understands what you're going through if you need a sympathetic ear.

Katie, a research scientist (names and details are disguised in examples throughout the guide), suffered for several years under a supervisor who treated her with contempt. Katie had been recruited into her plum position by her boss's boss, so she assumed that her boss resented her for that reason. Not wanting to make waves, she kept quiet and tried to do a good job. But then a chance conversation with one of his former direct reports led her to realize that the guy didn't hate *her*—he was generally a bad manager and grumpy guy. That gave Katie the courage to stand up to him in one-on-one meetings. "It was so helpful to realize that it wasn't just me," Katie recalls. "I stopped taking it personally and started thinking about how to get him to back off instead."

Network with his peers

Make sure your manager's peers know how hard you work and how much you care about the company. If your boss isn't giving you opportunities to demonstrate that to others, you'll need to do it by slowly building your own relationships with people in a position of influence, says Insead leadership professor Herminia Ibarra. Start by getting to know a couple of people outside your immediate group. The relationships can be casual—based initially on chitchat about movies or hobbies—or you can ask for formal introductions. Do a six-degrees-of-separation exercise if you can't think of an easy way to connect: Who in my circle can introduce me to this person?

One ally isn't enough, even if it's someone with lots of power. No matter how well placed that person is, your boss can damage your reputation with others in the company if you've got no one else in the senior ranks looking out for you.

Paula learned this the hard way. She emerged from a massive corporate reshuffle with her job intact and a new manager, Liz. Though Liz needed her expertise to get up and running, things between them quickly got rocky since Paula clearly had the CEO's ear. When the CEO asked Paula to handle a project for him on her own, Liz went into attack mode—criticizing her in public meetings, finding fault with her data. Paula saw the CEO's support as guaranteed job security, so she continued to work around Liz at his behest. But over time, Liz chipped away at her reputation—and the CEO's confidence in Paula eroded. She was eventually fired from the company.

Had Paula forged ties with a few influential people a level or two up, says leadership consultant Ron Ashkenas, she would have been less vulnerable to Liz's steady campaign against her.

Confront him

If you haven't managed to subtly change the dynamic with your boss, it might be time to speak openly with him about the problem. It's a risky move, but it could be your last, best chance to fix the situation, says Ashkenas. Don't have this conversation if you aren't prepared to switch jobs; it could backfire if your boss really does have it in for you. But in a case like that, you wouldn't want to stick around anyway.

Approach your boss in the most constructive way possible. Let him know that *you're on his side.* Say you want to find better ways to support him. No good will come of sulking with your arms folded or ranting about how unappreciated you are. Even if that's true, your boss won't respond calmly to that—he'll get defensive.

After you've set a positive tone by putting his needs front and center, make it clear that you're looking to grow, too. Explain that you're hoping to do that within the organization—ideally with his guidance. But say you'll also consider outside opportunities after a certain amount of time has passed (offer a reasonable time frame—maybe a year). To give him something concrete to work with, describe your big-picture professional goals and how you envision getting there. Suppose, for instance, you're eager to build your analytical skills: Volunteer to take on assignments that will require you to gather and interpret data. For example, you might comb through customer renewal rates to see if there are any patterns worth discussing. Ask your boss if he has other suggestions for developing those skills in your current role or if he'd recommend ways to get other senior managers in the company to see you in a new, high-potential light.

Of course, once your cards are on the table, be prepared for things not to go your way. But at least you'll have given yourself and your boss every opportunity to right the course.

Chapter 2
The Boss Who Pits You Against Your Colleagues

The Problem

Your boss has you competing against your peers for her respect and attention. It's a "reindeer games" scenario—only one of you can win some coveted prize, whether it's the chance to lead a team, a promotion, or just a moment in the limelight. She has created a horrible, cutthroat environment for an otherwise collegial group of direct reports.

Why It Happens

Though some bosses don't realize they're creating this problem, in many cases it's a deliberate management tactic: Task several people with solving a business challenge,

RETALIATION: ANDREA'S STORY

WHAT HAPPENED:

I worked in a small organization where two of us had the same title but very different jobs in practice. Our boss didn't see a problem with the ambiguity, but it created tension. I managed a team of people. My peer didn't manage anyone, but she had significant influence. She took every opportunity to undermine me by bad-mouthing me to my team. My direct reports would defend me, but it was rattling for them. In many cases, they'd come to me to tell me what was happening.

WHAT I DID:

I told my boss, and he said, "Don't worry, I'll take care of it." I assumed he spoke to her, because for two or three months, the behavior disappeared. But then she began sending around nasty e-mails about me—sometimes "inadvertently" copying me. Here's the really bad part: I figured out that people like that can be manipulated because they're convinced that others are actively working against them. So it was easy to fight back. I'd say things like, "I saw the owner of the company today, and we had a really good chat." That would freak her out. It implied that I was having some kind of exclusive conversation with the big boss. I wasn't—but she didn't know that. Ultimately her behavior got out of control, and she unspooled publicly. She got fired around the same time I left the company.

DID ANDREA GET IT RIGHT?

Andrea was effective, but at great cost to her colleague and herself. She allowed herself to slip down to her colleague's level—and it didn't make her any happier, just guiltier. She would have felt better taking a higher road, calling her colleague on the bad behavior and asking her boss to create more-distinct job titles and descriptions to clarify their responsibilities.

and make it an implicit horse race. Even when a promotion isn't on the table, senior executives often leave roles and responsibilities ambiguous as a test. They want to see who can take the pressure, who will rise to the occasion, who wants to get ahead badly enough to throw some sharp elbows.

Abraham Lincoln famously assembled a "team of rivals." He harnessed their competitive energy to bring out the best in each member and to produce the greatest results as a group. Bosses do the same. In some industries, such as investment banking and consulting, it's even considered a rite of passage, observes leadership consultant Jessica Pryce-Jones. The boss thinks, "I made *my* way to the top through healthy competition, so why shouldn't you?"

What to Do About It

An environment like this is frustrating for both you and your peers—and it can actually harm performance. When people focus intensely on beating one another out, they inevitably lose sight of larger goals and the greater good. Here are some ways to establish a friendlier, more collaborative dynamic—even when your boss (knowingly or not) sets the stage for conflict.

Make a pact

You and your colleagues can find your own ways of working together that don't ratchet up the competition. Leadership consultant Kathryn Heath figured this out early in her career, when an indifferent boss unwittingly set up a rivalry between Heath and a coworker. "We were in two different areas," Heath recalls, "but we needed to work together. Our boss didn't make roles and decision rights clear for us, so we had to sort them out ourselves." The colleague wanted to take the lead, just tapping Heath for whatever support he needed. But Heath didn't intend to play a supporting role. In fact, her colleague relied on re-sources *she* controlled.

Rather than engage in passive-aggressive games, Heath decided to have a straightforward discussion with him about how they could work together on a level field. "It was a tough conversation," she recalls, "because we were held accountable for different things." They tried to keep emotion out of it by focusing on coming to an understanding that would benefit both of their teams. "We came up with a detailed plan for how we'd handle certain situations. And we agreed to not make any big commitments or moves without talking to each other first." It wasn't a perfect solution, but by dealing with the issue directly, they diffused what could have been an incendiary relationship.

Establish ground rules, advises Susan Heathfield, an organizational development and HR expert. What if your colleague is playing dirty—by one-upping you in meetings, for example, or leaving you out of the loop so that you'll look clueless? Describe exactly what you see him doing, and ask him to stop. You may not feel comfortable confronting him, but work up the courage to do it. He'll be more likely to play fair in the future because he probably doesn't enjoy confrontation any more than you do. "He usually gets away with his behavior," says Heathfield, "so it's key to call him on it. If you allow it to continue unchecked, that trains him to do it more often—or to more of an extreme."

Call a time-out

You don't have to duke it out just because your boss has thrown you and a colleague in the ring. You can refuse to fight. Mary Davis Holt, one of Heath's partners, learned this in a past job—but not as soon as she'd have liked. Her boss had put her on a project with someone without making clear assignments, and it created conflict. Though Holt and her colleague had sat down in the beginning to sort out who would do what, over time she realized that she had allowed herself to do 80% of the work while her colleague was happy to claim credit for leading the effort.

"I probably should have recognized the imbalance earlier," she says. "But I was so eager for the next promotion, I wanted to show my willingness to go with the flow and be a flexible team player." The more she put up with, the more she saw her colleague as an adversary. In hindsight, what does she wish she'd done? Though she's glad she didn't let her anger erupt into a nasty fight over division of labor, she says, "I should have asked my boss to clarify our respective responsibilities right away." Once she spoke up and her boss realized what he'd set in motion, he agreed to step in to better divide the tasks.

Manage up

Tell your boss how you feel about the situation, but be diplomatic and constructive. If she thinks you're grousing, she won't take your concerns seriously. Or she might conclude that you have difficulty getting along with others (see chapter 4, "The Boss's Pet"). Discuss it with your colleague first, advises Heathfield—and then meet with your boss, perhaps together. Say you'd both like to stop vying for the spotlight because it's distracting you from doing your best work. Ask if she can avoid putting you in competitive situations (and give a few examples, in case she's not tuned in to the competition) so that you can both be more productive—to the benefit of all.

Some bosses think fostering internal competition helps them identify the truly talented, "like some kind of Darwinian gauntlet," says Pryce-Jones. She recently advised a junior investment banker who faced that problem. His boss tried to pit him directly against another colleague: Whoever had recommended the best-performing investments by the end of six months would be the "winner." The prize? The boss's favor—and job security. So the fledgling banker approached his boss with a different idea: Could he and his colleague work *together* to come up with the best picks? He identified reasons that would be better for the company, citing research about the benefits of collaboration. The boss agreed to try the experiment, and he's been pleased with the results. In Pryce-Jones's experience, this example isn't an outlier. "Most bosses are open to trying a different tack," she says. "Especially when you say, 'Here's how you could get more out of me.'"

Chapter 3
The Control-Freak Boss

The Problem

Your boss is smothering you. At first, you thought, "It's because I'm new—that's why he insists on reviewing every document before I distribute it and sitting in on all my meetings." But now that you're no longer learning your role, the tight leash feels downright oppressive and embarrassing. The other day, he actually scolded you for having a hallway chat with one of his peers about an idea you've been kicking around. You're hardworking, competent, smart. How are you ever going to escape your boss's shadow?

Why It Happens

Your boss is acting this way for a reason—though he may not be aware of it. Think about what could be driving his behavior. Try to get past the easy answer—it's probably not that he's evil or that he truly wants to keep you from being successful. Rather, his actions might be explained by factors that have little to do with you, such as a poor understanding of his role as manager, a micromanaging boss of his own, a lack of motivation to question how he's always done things, or personal insecurity.

What to Do About It

"Few people get the guidance they need to become good managers," says Carol Walker, a principal at Prepared to Lead, "and just about all of them have some insecurities about their competence. Accepting this may help you feel a little less frustrated with your boss. It's likely he's simply a flawed human being who thinks he is doing his best."

It can be hard to see things that way when your boss isn't cutting *you* any slack. His harping about every small misstep you take can feel overwhelmingly personal. But you don't have to resign yourself to being nitpicked to death. "You can't change your boss," Walker says, "but you have more power to improve the situation than you probably realize. It must be a process, not an event. It's a process that *you* have to own and direct."

Avoid his panic buttons

Form an educated guess about where your boss's sensitivities lie. If you believe, for example, that he's intimidated by those above him, think of ways you can alleviate that pressure, such as running reports to better prepare him for meetings with his manager. Or perhaps he's afraid that people don't perceive him as essential, and he's on a tear to prove how much you and others need him. Dispel his fears, advises communication and branding expert Dorie Clark, author of *Reinventing You*. Show him that you value his guidance. Ask him for feedback. Bring him any news you hear, and take your ideas to him before sharing them with others. As your boss begins to trust that you'll come to him without prompting, he may loosen his grip.

Once you get to know him better, you'll gain more insight into the areas he's touchy about. Looking at what has set him off historically—budget surprises? schedule changes?—will help you find ways of putting him at ease now, says Clark. Then you can assemble a dashboard to keep your boss as informed as he wants to be. Agree on your top priorities and the metrics that will demonstrate progress, and ask him how often he'd like to receive updates.

Your proactive, tailored-to-him system will comfort him. That's important, since micromanaging often stems from a boss's insecurity. "I call it 'snoopervising,'" says Stewart Tubbs, former dean of the College of Business at Eastern Michigan University. Turn the behavior around by preempting it: Tell your boss you want him to feel he can count on you and your work. Frequently report to him on your progress—before he can even think to check up on you. And use language that signals active listening. Tubbs recalls one young man who said "Consider it done" at the end of every meeting with his boss. Another young woman said "Understood" to show that she was engaged and on board. This isn't about simply placating your boss, notes Tubbs. You have to earn his trust by performing well. These employees consistently delivered, so over time their verbal reassurance meant something and helped their bosses relax.

Don't fight it

If you openly rebel against micromanagement, Clark cautions, your boss may clamp down even more. Leadership consultant Ron Ashkenas agrees. Instead of viewing it as a blow to your ego, he suggests, think about how you might actually benefit from it. Your boss may have your best interests in mind. Perhaps he wants to ensure that you have a sound understanding of the company's protocol or the most effective ways to work the system to get things done.

Regardless of the cause, says Ashkenas, accept that your boss may have something important to teach you. Just try to learn as much as you can, as quickly as you can—in case he doesn't eventually let up and you decide you can't take it anymore.

Scrutinize yourself

If your boss doesn't appear to have faith in your ability to do your job, consider whether you've given him a reason to feel this way. Have you missed important deadlines? Delivered presentations that fell flat? Assembled proposals that failed to win business? Take a hard look at yourself—and look around. If your boss isn't micromanaging other colleagues, his behavior could be a clue that you're underperforming.

If you suspect that's the case, ask him about it, says Clark. Tell him you feel he's monitoring you extra closely and you want to understand what's behind it. Is there a particular area where he feels you need guidance? Some bosses are reluctant to be straight with employees about their shortcomings, especially if criticism might be met with hostility. They may go to extremes, such as overly aggressive monitoring, to avoid having awkward conversations. So make it easier for your boss: Say you're genuinely interested in feedback on your weaknesses, even if it's hard to hear. Stay calm as you listen to the feedback (don't even let a grimace cross your face). Once you get a clear sense of where you stand, you'll have a better shot at addressing his concerns.

Thank your boss for his insights and tell him that you want to come back to him with an improvement plan. You might need to soothe your ego for a day or two, but the sooner you return to him with a proposal, the more seriously he'll take you. Ask if he can recommend potential mentors (inside or outside the company). See if human resources might help by suggesting a course to develop your project management or public speaking skills. If you approach the conversation openly—and then earnestly work on your shortcomings—you'll likely find your boss trusting you more and more.

Look ahead

Focusing on your future may help you and your boss interact more productively in the present. So initiate a discussion about your long-term professional goals. Set up a one-on-one meeting, or ask if you can use one of your scheduled check-ins to talk about your role. Explain that you want to start communicating

MICROMANAGED: LUKE'S STORY

WHAT HAPPENED:

After I'd worked for years at a large company, my two bosses moved me to a small division to run the trouble child: a start-up that had already cycled through three directors in two years. My bosses had many other people reporting to them, but I was their chief focus because the new venture had already burned through a lot of money on an untested model. They micromanaged like crazy. They had no idea what would work, so they tried 10 new things a week, yanking the team this way and that. I realized pretty quickly that my job was to manage them, to serve as a heat shield in hopes of keeping my staff on something resembling a plan.

But I wasn't able to do that at our staff lunches at the end of each week, when everyone in the division piled into a large conference room to share updates and brainstorm ideas. The room was filled with both senior and junior staff. Anything could set off my more volatile boss, whose sidekick would then join him in publicly stomping me or my managers to a pulp over a perceived lapse in procedure or strategy. When the controller couldn't spit out numbers fast enough to answer any and all questions fired at him—what do we know about X this week?— he was pummeled, and then so was I for not having him prepare properly for the meeting. And on it went, week after week. I would spend each weekend scrambling to contain whatever damage had been done or rushing off to the next fire that the bosses had declared our New Top Priority. These lunches were, of course, in addition to daily floggings, plus phone calls night and day (Sunday, 7 AM: "Why didn't you know this server was down since 4 AM?").

WHAT I DID:

Finally, after two years of this, my beleaguered controller and I hit upon one number that hadn't yet been questioned: How much had we spent on these lunches? When I mentioned the number in a cost-cutting discussion, suddenly the lunches went from weekly to biweekly. Then monthly. Then not at all. I didn't cure my bosses of their management styles. But at least I managed to take some of the sting out of my week.

DID LUKE GET IT RIGHT?

Luke probably couldn't have diffused his bosses' control-freak tendencies altogether in such a highly charged situation—the running of a troubled start-up division. But he was savvy in using costs, an issue they cared about deeply, to get them to drop the painful, unproductive lunches. Luke could have also tried to get ahead of their expectations. Knowing they saw such meetings as opportunities to grill employees on the spot, Luke could have used the time to showcase how his staff was on top of problems. And he could have met with his boss privately in advance to suss out areas of concern and then prepared his staff to address them with metrics or analysis. Finally, he could have proposed cost-control measures on a monthly or quarterly basis, because he knew his bosses would always respond favorably to that sort of discussion.

more regularly—and explicitly—about your growth and about how else you could support the department. Give him some examples of the types of projects you'd like to work on and the future role you envision for yourself. Say you're ready for more independence, and you'd like some opportunities to demonstrate that. Emphasize how important his feedback is to your growth. Offer some ideas on how you might realize your vision—and see if he can suggest others.

Keep the conversation constructive and forward-looking. Complaining about the past won't open your boss's mind or make him want to support you, Walker says. Being positive and taking ownership will. Let him know that you appreciate his guidance, but you're eager to spread your wings a little, too.

Ashkenas says junior colleagues at his firm have had this conversation with him—and it's worked well. He admits he struggles to fight his own micromanager tendencies. "I don't think I'm a control freak, but I do have strong feelings about quality," he says. His colleagues were subtle, but he understood what they were getting at ("Ron, do you still want to see the final slides and documents in advance?" "Would it be all right if I worked directly with the client to finish these?"). When people have diplomatically pointed this out to him, he's been happy to find ways to step back—once they've demonstrated that they can meet his quality standards.

Ease your boss's fears by emphasizing that you're willing to take this in steps. Chances are, he'll welcome your enthusiastic, respectful approach—not resist it. If he does resist, there's little point in fighting, Ashkenas says. "If your boss isn't ready or willing to let go, it might take more time for him to trust you and have confidence." You can revisit the subject down the line. Or, Ashkenas says, it might be possible that his need for being involved is so deep-seated and emotional that it will never change.

If your boss is receptive, however, thank him. But that meeting is just the beginning. Offer to update him on your progress at your regular check-ins, advises Walker. Use those meetings to share your thinking with him—not just what you're going to do but *why*. Ultimately your boss has to trust not only that you'll follow his instructions but also that you'll tackle problems in a way he approves. Close each meeting by proposing next steps and getting his buy-in.

Develop other champions

If your boss is micromanaging you, others may notice and start questioning your skills. That's why it's critical to build relationships outside his ken. "It's so important not to have all your eggs in one basket. Have points of contact with other people who can see your good work," says leadership expert Herminia Ibarra. You want them to get to know you and see what you're capable of when you're unfettered by your controlling boss.

Join interdepartmental committees, and get involved in cross-disciplinary pursuits. Organize a companywide volunteer day or a brown-bag lunch series that brings industry luminaries into your office. But avoid dabbling in areas where your boss considers himself the expert: He might feel upstaged by your efforts and pull the plug on them—or try to insinuate himself. Tell him what you'd like to do *before* you volunteer so that you don't take him by surprise and trigger his instinct to micromanage.

Chapter 4
The Boss's Pet

The Problem

Your boss has a pet employee who gets the most interesting assignments and special perks, such as flextime and an expense account. She invites her pet to social events, confides inappropriately to him about "problem" colleagues, and acts like they're old friends. And she doesn't seem to hold him to the same standards that apply to the rest of your team: You all log in extra hours and go above and beyond, while he appears to just coast along. It drives you crazy.

Why It Happens

Sometimes favoritism is actually fair: The pet has a burning talent and desire to excel, works hard without complaining, and shares the boss's goals and vision. Understandably, the boss is high on her star performer.

But what if she favors an average performer? In that case, her pet is just a buddy. Like everyone else, your boss enjoys having friends at work. So she may latch on to an employee she sees as a kindred spirit—someone with whom she's comfortable. Or perhaps she's inherited a direct report she's already friends with outside of work.

BEST IN SHOW: ALICE'S STORY

WHAT HAPPENED:

When I started my first job as a journalist at a magazine in New York, I swiftly realized that my boss—the maker or breaker of careers there—favored people with the "right" pedigree. He was far more impressed by someone with an Ivy League degree and Park Avenue parents than by a summa cum laude who'd put herself through a state school. For the first few months, I gnashed my teeth as I watched one of my peers—I'll call him Yale boy— get assignments and opportunities that were clearly above our entry-level position. The boss just treated Yale boy differently.

WHAT I DID:

After spending weeks complaining to my roommate about how unfair it was, I realized something: My boss didn't really know me yet. He didn't know what I was capable of doing. So of course he initially favored the guy with the same credentials he had—at that point, there was little else for him to go on. But over time, I established my skills and ambition. I threw myself into my job. I volunteered for assignments I knew I'd learn from rather than waiting for my boss to hand me growth opportunities. I also worked at building my internal network. One Sunday afternoon, my boss called the office, and I happened to be there, picking up some files. When I answered the phone, he was clearly pleased that I was working that hard. He said, "That's how people get ahead in this company." And that was true. I was promoted pretty soon after that—and Yale boy didn't stick around long enough to achieve the same.

DID ALICE GET IT RIGHT?

Once Alice stopped obsessing about her peer and started focusing on what she could control—her own development and performance—things fell into place for her. She proved to her boss that she had the skills and dedication he was looking for, and the pet's pedigree ceased to get in her way.

"Buddy" pets often take advantage of their status to obtain benefits for themselves. For example, they might ask for extra vacation days, off the record. Or they might turn a casual lunch or drinks after work into an opportunity to gain an insider's perspective, pressing for details about meetings above his pay grade and asking what the boss thinks of others in the group.

When your boss plays along, it can really stick in your craw—but don't let it.

What to Do About It

Build your own positive relationship with your boss instead of looking for ways to dethrone the pet. That's how you'll get the resources and attention you want without picking—and losing—a fight.

Stop obsessing

There's little point to moaning that your boss has a favorite and it's not fair. That's not going to change the situation. In fact, it could make things worse. "You'll just look like you're whining," says leadership consultant Jill Flynn. Both your boss and your colleagues may see it as evidence that you have trouble getting along with others (see chapter 2, "The Boss Who Pits You Against Your Colleagues"). Your boss may not want to assign you to projects with her pet for fear that you won't play nicely. And the pet might pick up your negative vibe and steer clear of you—effectively making you a pariah.

Get to know your boss

It's not sucking up to ask your boss how her weekend went or to compare notes on restaurants you'd like to try.

As Kent Lineback, coauthor of *Being the Boss*, points out, your relationship with your boss is as much a reflection of what you put into it as what your boss does, so invest time in getting to know her. Ask about the article she's writing. Invite her to coffee or lunch, without an agenda.

As a manager, I liked it when someone on my team suggested going out for lunch just to chat. Even when I was too busy to accept, I always appreciated the invitation. Bosses enjoy sharing stories about their families and vacations as much as anyone else. So cut your boss some slack and reach out to her. You may not replace her "pet," but you'll create goodwill.

Of course, even if your relationship with your boss becomes friendlier, she's still your boss. If you try to get too chummy, she may see you as a sycophant. Colleagues may think you're angling to be the new pet and start gossiping.

Communication and branding expert Dorie Clark says not to lose sight of decorum—especially when connecting through social media. If you (or your friends) post with abandon on Facebook, think twice about "friending" your boss. You can follow her on Twitter (or suggest that she follows you, if you're a prolific tweeter) as long as you keep it professional: Comment on news stories and industry trends, share useful articles recommended by members of your network, that kind of thing. This may help your boss realize that you've made smart contacts and you're in tune with important ideas.

Shine your own light

Many people are reluctant to draw attention to their successes, leadership consultant Kathryn Heath points out. "They don't talk about their accomplishments in the first person. They say 'the team did this' instead of 'I led the team doing this.'"

Does this sound like you? If so, Heath advises getting over your modesty if you don't want the pet to consume all your boss's attention: "You can speak diplomatically, but make your contributions clear." Your busy manager may be so focused on his own challenges that he fails to notice all the good work you do. So you'll have to toot your horn a little. "Give others credit where it's due," Heath says, "but take your own credit, too."

When Heath recently reviewed a presentation that a coaching client was planning to make to her boss, she noted that the woman used "team" language to describe work she had done to win a big assignment from a new customer. Heath pointed it out, and her client revised the presentation, saying she had cultivated the customer relationship and identified the right people to help win the job. Instead of allowing her contribution to be swallowed up by a faceless team-player credit, "she told a very compelling story and got promoted."

Women tend to find this particularly difficult, Heath says, based on hundreds of 360-degree reviews that she and her colleagues have conducted. They want their performance to speak for itself. If I do good work, they think, it will be noticed—people will consider me for great assignments because I'm so productive and reliable.

Unfortunately, that's not how it works. If you want to be top of mind, you need to boost your visibility. When you attend a conference, for example, send your boss a list of 10 takeaways you'd like to share with the team when you return. You'll impress her with your initiative and team focus. And schedule a regular check-in with your boss to discuss your priorities and the progress you've made on them. At annual review time, provide a summary of your year, highlighting key accomplishments, before your boss does her write-up. This will make it easy for her to remember what you did a few months ago, too, not just your recent achievements. The meetings and documentation will serve as reminders that her pet isn't her only valuable contributor.

It's possible to make a positive impression on your boss without irritating your colleagues or behaving in a way that doesn't feel authentic to you, says organizational development and HR expert Susan Heathfield. Transform yourself into an indispensable employee. Ask for more challenging assignments. Raise your hand for projects that others don't want to do. Don't just alert your boss to problems she'll need to solve; suggest solutions. Be a team builder—tap the strengths of your coworkers, praise them when they make good contributions, elevate the discourse of the entire organization. "So often bosses are subjected to complaints," says Heathfield. "If you rise above the nonsense, that's a really good place to be."

There's a standout employee in Heathfield's own company who voluntarily mentors junior staff members, organizes social functions, and gives people in other departments a hand when she can—for instance, by helping HR screen candidates in early-stage interviews. She's approachable, knowledgeable, and trustworthy. "She's just a go-to person," Heathfield observes. "She never comes across as self-promotional. She's always focused on what would be best for *the company*." That's why no one begrudges her success or wants to see her fall from grace. It's also why she's been promoted twice in recent years—and she's on senior managers' high-potential list.

Chapter 5
The Disaffected Boss

The Problem

Your boss has "checked out." He's there physically but not in spirit. He doesn't meet regularly with your group or bother to fill any of you in on the critical decisions that senior management is wrestling with. So you're often the last ones to hear about big initiatives and changes. He doesn't fight for resources, raises, or promotions for your team—or seem to care about his people at all. If he's given up on his career, fine, but he's essentially giving up on yours, too. He's practically invisible in the organization, and you're at a loss for how to get anyone to notice your contributions so that you can advance.

Why It Happens

Some bosses become so consumed with lining up the Next Big Thing on their impressive rise to the top that they lose interest in their present roles. Others disengage as managers when they sense that their *own* futures are limited. Feeling embittered toward their companies, they may passive-aggressively refuse to manage and view that as payback for all the wrongs they've endured. They stop jockeying for budget dollars, perk allocations, new-hire slots, and so on—and quietly allow performance to fizzle out as a result.

It's also common for a boss to start phoning it in near the end of his career. People burn out over time, especially in high-pressure roles. If that's the case with your manager, he may no longer have the energy to care—and he's probably just biding his time until he can leave to focus on his photography and gardening.

Whatever the reason, it's probably not about you. It's all about him.

What to Do About It

When your boss lacks drive and commitment, it can be hard to see the upside. But you may actually benefit from his disinterest. It gives you a chance to fill the void with your own good work. If he doesn't seem to care about much of anything, then he's not likely to mind if you find ways to step in and raise your own profile, as long as your efforts don't make more work for him. Of course, you're probably on your own to figure out *what* to do. Here are some guidelines.

Try speaking up

Sometimes bosses just need a little prompting, says Boston University management professor Kathy Kram.

STEPPING UP: JOHN'S STORY

WHAT HAPPENED:

In hindsight, I think I was hired because my boss had already checked out. He'd been in charge of a key division of a small private company for nearly two decades. I later learned that he'd asked the owner for equity and been denied. But the owner trusted and valued him, and my boss knew his job was safe. Essentially, he brought me in to do his job—or to make his job as easy as possible. I was hired as a number two. My boss, it soon became clear, didn't work the same hours as the rest of us. He'd blame traffic patterns for coming in midmorning. And he'd spend a lot of days "working from home." I didn't really mind, for the most part. It made my job easy and fun. He stayed out of my way, and I ran the division.

WHAT I DID:

I just tried to make him look good whenever possible, knowing it would give the owner confidence that things were being run smoothly and make my boss trust me.

We happily bumped along like that for a few years, until the owner of the company decided to sell. Then my boss kicked back into gear. I think he wanted to impress prospective owners and possibly get that equity stake he'd longed for. Suddenly he became deeply involved and dithered over every decision. He second-guessed things I'd done for years that hadn't bothered him before. I ended up feeling like I couldn't quite get it right anymore with him. When the company was sold, he didn't manage to impress the new ownership team. He resigned shortly thereafter. I stayed on long enough to find a decent new job, but I ultimately chose to leave, too.

DID JOHN GET IT RIGHT?

John was in a tough position, but he made the most of it. In some ways, he'd been given a dream job: He was the acting boss, without the bottom-line responsibility. He could learn, experiment, and develop without anyone breathing down his neck. But working for a disaffected boss isn't really a long-term career strategy. Even if the company hadn't changed hands, something else would have put an end to this unspoken agreement. His boss might have retired, or John may have decided he wanted the responsibility after all, not just the freedom.

"I've seen managers and employees in my class who say, 'I just wish my boss would meet with me more often, give me more feedback...' I always pose the question 'Have you *asked* for that?' Very often, they haven't." Many bosses are oblivious to their employees' needs, Kram points out, but respond well to reasonable, diplomatic requests, especially if they're easy to grant.

Make delegation attractive

Volunteer to take on tasks your disengaged boss doesn't enjoy, suggests Stewart Tubbs, former dean of the College of Business at Eastern Michigan University. You don't want him to take offense or resent your ambition and energy—so how do you gently encourage him to delegate to you? Invite him to coffee or lunch, says Tubbs, and ask if you can do anything to lighten his workload, even on a trial basis. Say you're eager to learn new skills. Frame it as a win-win—you want to help him out and grow in the process. Most bosses would welcome the opportunity to delegate to a *willing* taker, says Tubbs, especially if you promise to send completed projects or reports to him first so that he can decide with whom and how to share them.

Fill in the gaps

Show your boss that cultivating your talents will give the team more muscle—with little or no extra effort on his part. Offer to learn new technologies, for example, or to do first drafts of reports he's responsible for. Have a good relationship with Manny in finance? Work with him to file the team's expense reports so that your boss won't have to. Sharpen the skills you know that he lacks; he might see it as a lifeboat.

Tubbs knew a young woman who got on her indifferent boss's good side by creating outstanding PowerPoint presentations. Before long, he was asking for her help with all his slides, and eventually he invited her to do some of the presenting. Once other leaders in the company saw her skills in action, they started tapping her for presentations, too. When the company later went through a severe downsizing, she was one of the few people who still had a job, primarily because her boss had come to rely on her so much. The same principle can apply to spreadsheets, social media, and so on. You may need to offer your assistance several times before the timing is right, Tubbs advises. But sooner or later, your boss will be so busy, he'll accept your offer. Do your best work when he asks you to step into the breach—you'll increase your chances of scoring repeat opportunities.

Build your own network

You probably already realize how critical it is to build relationships with colleagues, since your boss isn't doing that on behalf of your team. But he may actually be a good source of inspiration when you're deciding which people to add to your network and how to reach out to them.

Here's what communication and branding expert Dorie Clark suggests: "You might say something like 'Look, I'm really committed to the company, really interested in expanding my knowledge and working my way toward a senior role in the marketing department. But I need some guidance on networking to make that happen. What advice would you give me?'" Your boss may surprise you with helpful ideas. Few people are so emotionally disengaged that they won't respond to a flattering request like this. "But don't just wait for the pearls of wisdom to drop," Clark adds. "Ask specific questions: 'If I want to develop strengths in X, which people do I need to talk to?' 'Who in the company really excels in that area?'"

Your boss may not go to bat for his team on a day-to-day basis, but if you engage him in a big-picture conversation about your development, he may be inclined to share contacts or ideas. It's a low-effort way for him to give you meaningful help. Ask if he'll introduce you to people he's named or if he'll keep an eye out for opportunities where you could gain more related experience, now that he knows your long-term plans.

Even if your boss can't quite muster the motivation to make introductions, you'll at least come away with a name or two. You can then create your own opportunities to meet or work with those people by volunteering for committees they work on, for example, and taking time to chat with them at lunch. Sometimes personal ties that start in cafeteria lines evolve into supportive professional relationships.

As you're working on those internal relationships, you'll want to cultivate external ones, too. Research shows that creating connections beyond your company is critical to building a robust network, says leadership expert Herminia Ibarra. That's because they exponentially increase your awareness of job opportunities in other organizations and industries, your chances of being recruited, and your ability to find mentors and allies with whom you can safely discuss career hopes and challenges. Ask colleagues if they know people outside work with expertise or knowledge you're trying to acquire—and if they do, don't be afraid to ask for introductions.

Section 2
Political Challenges with Your Colleagues

Chapter 6
The Hypercompetitive Peer

The Problem

There's one in every office: a colleague who is so competitive, so obnoxious, that she stops at nothing to get every advantage over her peers. She brags about her successes, races to be first in line for high-profile projects, weasels out of grunt work, and consistently "forgets" to mention anyone else's contributions when she's praised for something that's really a team effort. She's dead set on getting ahead, even at the expense of everyone else.

Why It Happens

People become overly competitive at work for two reasons (assuming they aren't just jerks), says leadership and networking expert Brian Uzzi at Northwestern's Kellogg School of Management. Often they feel they have to fight for limited resources, such as promotions, raises, or travel. Or they may view you as a threat. "Maybe you have fresh ideas, or you do especially well in front of clients. You do something better than your peer does," Uzzi explains. "If the other person wasn't threatened by you, he or she wouldn't waste time competing."

What to Do About It

Rivalries can be deeply destructive to your career. You'll be unhappy in an environment where you have overtly or subtly hostile relationships. And you might signal to your superiors that you aren't leadership material if you get caught up in a cold war at work. Here's how to avoid the drama and the damage that comes with it:

Give her the benefit of the doubt

Thinking about your peer as hypercompetitive is actually part of the problem, says Diana McLain Smith, author of *The Elephant in the Room: How Relationships Make or Break the Success of Leaders and Organizations.* Smith points out that individuals behave better or worse depending on the relationship patterns they unwittingly create with one another. So, for example, if you view someone as a competitor, you'll treat her as one. And, in turn, she'll *feel* more competitive toward you. Your behavior will feed hers. This isn't to say that people don't have characteristic ways of behaving—a competitive person will naturally be so in all kinds of situations. "But relationships have the power to amplify or modify those ways of behaving," Smith says. Her advice? "Act as if" you believe the other person wants to succeed, but not necessarily at your expense. That trick of mind will stop you from doing things that could trigger or escalate an arms race, such as overreacting to a slight, one-upping her at meetings, or trying to undermine her before she undermines you.

Also consider whether you've accidentally done anything to provoke the attacks. It may seem to you that she's "just" launching into you, but an abundance of social-cognitive research shows that we're blind to our parts in these encounters. Ask a trusted colleague for a reality check. You may discover a trigger that you can easily avoid in the future.

Address the root of the problem

What if you find that you're not provoking the behavior? You'll need to figure out what's causing the competition, says Uzzi. By considering your peer's point of view and understanding what's behind her actions, you may be able to come up with a solution that eases the tension.

Suppose you're both associates trying to make partner at your firm. If just a few slots are open to new partners, competition is baked into the career track—your peer isn't to blame for it. In a case like that, Uzzi suggests approaching key decision makers to try to fix the problem at its root. You could talk to current partners before they've decided on the next crop of promotions, for example. Frame the conversation constructively: You've identified a problem, and you'd like to help address it. Maybe the cutthroat environment has led employees to leave your firm and join others. Point to those losses, and quantify their impact on the top or bottom line, to show how important it is to stop the bleeding. Ask if there's any flexibility in the promotion cycle: For instance, can the firm add two partners in one year and none the next to retain two superstars and give others time to develop their portfolios? If you and your rival are clearly assets to the company, decision makers should be receptive to a conversation like this. It's in their best interest, not just yours.

Call in friendly reinforcements

Still having problems? "What I've seen people do effectively is to band together with other colleagues," says leadership consultant Ron Ashkenas. "If there's one highly ambitious person annoying you and playing political games, she's probably also doing it to other people." Ashkenas advises gently approaching the competitive colleague with one or two peers (not a large gang—that would get her defenses up). Perhaps take her out for coffee. Your conversation should be friendly. Ask if she realizes she's been sending off a competitive vibe. "Be as specific as possible," Ashkenas says. "Give examples. If she takes it reasonably well, offer to speak up in the moment so that she can see when it's happening." Sometimes simply making a competitive colleague aware of how others perceive her behavior is enough to change the pattern.

Don't take the bait

If your colleague makes the competition public—in meetings or with your boss, for example—it's critical to keep calm, advises communication and branding expert

Dorie Clark. "It will become clear to other people that she has some kind of agenda," Clark says. "Don't participate in the rivalry." If you do, you'll only fuel your colleague's ambition further and perhaps lower others' estimation of you. And, if you're spending emotional energy worrying about how you stack up against her, you won't have enough left to do your job well.

That's not to say you should let her batter you or your reputation—you'll just invite more of the same (see chapter 7, "The Bully"). Suppose your colleague Barb calls your work "irrelevant" in a staff meeting, says Smith: "I'd be prepared to respond—both publicly and one-on-one with Barb afterward."

At the meeting, you might ask dispassionately, "What makes you say so?" If she claims your logic is flawed and you've no solid data to back it up, calmly respond: "Perhaps you've missed the data and analysis on pages 5 and 6." And if she insists that the numbers don't support your case, you can say—again, in a controlled, even tone—"I realize that's your view, but saying something is irrelevant doesn't make it so. I'd be interested to hear what others think of the data and analysis."

And privately, here's how you might put her on notice: "Barb, it's hard for me to see how calling my work irrelevant would ever serve the team or even you. If anything, it makes you look bad. What was that all about?" She might surprise you with a contrite response—or she might refuse to acknowledge her behavior. Either way, you've established that you're not an easy target and that attacking you probably isn't worth her effort.

DOUBLE-CROSSED: JANET'S STORY

WHAT HAPPENED:

I'd been given the top position in my group at a relatively young age—I wasn't even 30, and my peers in other divisions were all in their 40s. So I brought in a highly ambitious number two to shore up areas where I didn't have as much expertise. On paper, Matt, my number two, looked like a better fit for certain aspects of my job, but I knew my boss trusted me and wanted me in the position. About a year in, I thought I'd built a great relationship with Matt. I'd given him lots of freedom, responsibility, and visibility, and I'd learned a lot from watching and working with him. But then a senior executive pulled me aside to tell me that Matt had gone to the top boss and asked for my job. I was flabbergasted and hurt. In hindsight, I realized that my letting him "shine" had allowed him to take sole credit for things and position himself as the real power player in the department.

WHAT I DID:

I called Matt into my office, closed the door (rare at our company), and told him I knew. After he stammered through an explanation that he was just expressing his ambition, I voiced my disappointment: I'd prided myself on helping him grow, and I certainly never intended to hold him back—but now he'd lost my trust. He left my office with his head hanging. I knew his ambitions wouldn't diminish, but from that point on, I didn't let him take the spotlight nearly as much. I made presentations without him. Held meetings without him. Treated him more like a direct report than a partner. Not surprisingly, he soon left the company for a prominent position in a start-up.

DID JANET GET IT RIGHT?

Tough call. Janet's decision to hire an openly ambitious number two had the potential to backfire. Janet was, in some ways, an ideal boss for Matt—it made sense to add his strengths to the bench and give him lots of room to grow. But she also had a hand in creating the problem. Self-conscious that she didn't have some of his particular expertise, she stepped *too* far out of the picture, allowing him to elbow his way past her. She looked weak, not like a confident boss who was delegating. And she should have had an open conversation with Matt early on about his ambitions and helped him chart a career path. That way, he would have viewed her as a catalyst rather than an obstacle.

Charm and disarm

If you sense that your competitive colleague feels threatened by you, find ways to support her. Say, for example, you're an academic with a gift for teaching, and your peer struggles in the classroom but does superb research. Suggest teaming up so that you can work together toward earning tenure. "Tell your colleague you'd like his or her input on your course materials," Uzzi suggests. "Or offer to have him sit in on one of your classes to provide feedback. You'll both benefit from a fresh eye and new ideas. Involving your peer in your work turns a rival into a collaborator. And a shared activity can build trust." By initiating some give-and-take, you can neutralize the perceived threat and, over time, transform the relationship into one of mutual respect.

Advocate for yourself

You can obsess about how horrible a competitor is—or you can focus on your own work and advancement. "In our firm," says executive coach Beth Weissenberger, "we see so many clients who get passed over for great jobs because their strategy was effectively 'I do a good job. Everyone should know that. My work will speak for itself.' But you're not going to be promoted if you keep your head down and steam about how unfair things are."

Weissenberger coached two high potentials who had this problem. Both had been flagged by their company as potential CFOs, but neither had articulated their career goals to their boss. So they risked losing out on chances to develop skills and gain visibility—those would go to people who spoke up and said they were looking for growth. "People need to know that you're ambitious," says Weissenberger, "as long as you don't express it in an obnoxious way. Does your boss even realize you want to be promoted? Everyone always assumes yes, but it's not always the case. You have to be very clear: 'I'm committed to doing this job well, but here's what I'm striving for. If you're looking for a future CFO candidate, I'd like to work toward the opportunity.'"

Chapter 7
The Bully

The Problem

Your colleague is a bully. When you're speaking in meetings, he doodles, sends e-mails, whispers to colleagues—to the point of distracting others, and sometimes even you, from what you're trying to say. He's also blown up at you in front of others for petty reasons. You dread interacting with him and find yourself constantly waiting for his next attack. You can't just brush it off, and it's ruining your focus at work. The specifics may sound silly to someone who's not experiencing this, but to you it feels like psychological harassment.

Why It Happens

Bullying in the workplace is not much different from what happens on the playground. Bullies of all ages want to manipulate the political and social power in their environment to control others. You'd think we'd outgrow it, but it's all too common in the office: In a 2010 Workplace Bullying Institute survey conducted by Zogby International, 35% of Americans reported being bullied at work. Why is the problem so widespread? People and organizations put up with the bad behavior, afraid to confront or penalize the culprits.

What to Do About It

Being bullied at work can wreak havoc on your mental and emotional health—and your performance on the job. This happens a lot, according to a study by Christine Pearson at the Thunderbird School of Global Management and Christine Porath at Georgetown University's McDonough School of Business: 78% of participants who believed they'd been treated rudely by colleagues said they felt a decreased commitment to their work, with a direct negative effect on their performance. You—and your work—don't have to suffer. These steps will help you change the dynamic.

Consider his intentions

Some bullies don't mean to be bullies. So make sure you aren't projecting a motive that isn't there. If, for example, a peer consistently criticizes you in public, think through what he might actually be trying to accomplish, suggests leadership consultant Ron Ashkenas. Is it possible he has honorable intentions? Is he being critical of *you* or just striving to ensure high quality?

Gut-check your feelings with a work friend, or discreetly ask a trusted colleague to sit in on a meeting where the problem usually arises. A neutral perspective may help you see that the bully is not out to get you. Perhaps he's insecure in a new role and overcompensating, for instance, or he lacks the emotional intelligence to see how cutting his words and actions are. If he doesn't realize how he's coming across, you can pull him aside and ask him if everything is OK. "You seemed angry about that report. Is there something we should talk about?" As with many of the political challenges in this guide, it's entirely possible that your colleague is so wrapped up in his own thoughts or anxieties that he has no idea how he behaves toward you. Simply mentioning it might make him more self-aware.

With third-party feedback, you may also realize it's not you; it's him. Knowing that, you can shrug off his bad behavior more easily. Bullies notoriously pick on people who appear weak and fragile. Show that you're not afraid of criticism and that you're willing to stand up for yourself, and your bully may well back down.

Offer an olive branch

Disarm your bully by expressing your desire to have a good relationship with him. If he's intentionally pushing you around, he's assuming you're his adversary. So show him that you want to be on the same team. If he routinely derails your project launches, approach him before the next one: Tell him how important his input is and that you appreciate his eye for potential obstacles. After you've set a constructive example, he may change his tune: "Maybe I should have come to you with my concerns *before* the last launch..." Even a small concession like that can be a first step toward a more productive working relationship, says communication and branding expert Dorie Clark.

Find safety in numbers

Although you don't want to create a rival gang to counter the office bully, there is power in people banding together to support one another publicly. If you notice your bully targeting others, too, tell them about the behavior you've observed and what you've experienced yourself. Discuss how you might join forces. You could agree to stand up for one another in moments of confrontation, for instance, or help one another anticipate and address the bully's criticisms. At the very least, you'll have others to turn to when you're feeling the need to vent.

Break the pattern

It's easy to get trapped in a negative pattern with a bully. He always does certain things, and you always respond in a certain way. Maybe you find yourself complaining to a colleague after every showdown. Or you try to outbully him by doing your own masterful doodles and rolling *your* eyes when *he* talks.

How do you put an end to this destructive dance? The easiest thing to change is your own behavior. Take a quick walk outside after a frustrating encounter. Or send a positive e-mail, such as a thank-you note or a compliment to another colleague you've been meaning to write. Break the cycle of negativity with something positive.

Call him on it

Book a one-on-one meeting with the bully. Public confrontation will only exacerbate his natural tendencies, so find a space where there's no audience. Bullies often bank on the fact that people won't call them on their behavior, so your initiating a meeting will get his attention.

Suppose your bully is passive-aggressive. He makes snide remarks under his breath, and you've heard from reliable sources that he's bad-mouthing your ideas to the rest of the team. Tell him you'd like to talk to him because you get the sense he's unhappy with the proposed process changes (or whatever he's grumbling about). Stick with the facts. Don't attack him, as in "You always do such and such..." Instead, be specific and neutral, Clark advises. Say something like, "In today's meeting, you were muttering to yourself when we went over the process proposal. I wanted to discuss it because the same thing happened at last week's meeting, and I'm concerned about the way we're interacting. Can we talk about how we're working together so that we can both be more effective?" Be direct, but give him the opportunity to express his point of view. Ask him how he thinks his concerns can be addressed.

The same technique works well for colleagues who are more blatantly disrespectful: "You asked some great questions this morning, but your tone was pretty harsh. I'm wondering, was there a problem?" Odds are, the bully will back down immediately because he doesn't want a confrontation. Your directness will serve as a warning: You noticed his behavior, and you're willing to address it. At a minimum, observes organizational development

PUBLIC FLOGGING: JASON'S STORY

WHAT HAPPENED:

When I first began working in a well-known global consulting firm, a senior colleague asked me to prepare data slides for an important client presentation. He gave me very specific, detailed instructions on what he wanted and then left for the night. When I reviewed the task, I thought I could do the same thing a lot more efficiently. So that's what I did.

The next day, as we were presenting the material to the client, he called up my data slides. When he saw I hadn't done it the way he'd asked, he just went nuts. He embarrassed me in front of the client and my peers. He even followed me back to my desk after the presentation to continue haranguing me. It was awful. But that was typical of the way he treated me the entire time we both worked there.

WHAT I DID:

I avoided him. I did no favors for him, never volunteered to help him, just tried to fade into the background as far as he was concerned. And I secretly celebrated each time he made a mistake. It didn't make him go away, but at least I kept my distance.

DID JASON GET IT RIGHT?

Jason might have turned things around if he'd shown more empathy for his colleague. Yes, this guy was a bully, but he'd received no heads-up about the slides—and he'd felt blindsided in front of a big client.

After the blowup, what if Jason had approached him privately, explained that he hadn't meant to do an end run, and asked if they could figure out a better way to communicate to avoid the same situation in the future? That approach might have earned his colleague's respect. And if not, it would at least have put his bully on notice: Jason wouldn't just slink away after a public flogging like that. He'd speak up.

and HR expert Susan Heathfield, it makes the bully think twice about targeting you in the future.

Go toe-to-toe with the bully

You don't need to simmer silently the next time your bully acts up. Peter Freeth, a director of UK-based Revelation Consulting, which specializes in high-performing cultures, advises his clients to calmly stand their ground during the attack: "He aggressively questions you? Ignore his questions. Absolutely ignore them. He whispers? He's drawing other people into his game. Stop and look directly at him. Continue only when he's quiet. When he does it again, stop and look. His behavior is disrespectful. You know it; everyone else knows it. The problem is that they're all too polite to do anything about it." You don't need to get caught up in retaliating. Simply take away his power to rattle you. He'll move on to another victim or perhaps put his energy toward something more useful.

Just say no

What if somebody more senior, such as your boss, is the one bullying you? You still have to draw a line. Otherwise, the entire relationship will take on a master-servant dynamic.

Leadership consultant Jessica Pryce-Jones describes a client who faced this problem—a very senior investment banker whose boss frequently made unreasonable demands on her. "He'd say, 'I want you in the office at 6:30 AM to look at my presentation.' Or 'I need to be able to reach you at 11:30 at night.'"

The banker was warm and helpful by nature. But she grew increasingly resentful when her boss started taking advantage of that. Pryce-Jones advised her to think about circumstances when she could reasonably say no— for instance, when preparing for an event would keep her awake at night. If a request seemed excessive by those standards, she needed to explain what she wouldn't do (by simply declining the request) and what she would do instead. Pryce-Jones encouraged her to try this out a few times and then evaluate how it felt. After declining a couple of such requests, she had a clearer sense of her boundaries—and she felt much less resentful. This gave her more energy for what she said *yes* to. Making active decisions empowered her and increased her confidence.

Work up the courage to say no a couple of times to make it clear that you aren't a pushover. Of course, if you worry about your job security or if your work environment becomes hostile, you should report it to human resources.

Chapter 8
The Clique

The Problem

There's a group of "golden" people in your office. They get assigned to high-profile projects, receive lots of public praise for their work, and ascend the ranks faster than others. They're a tight crowd: They have one another's backs in meetings and socialize after work. You've never been tapped to be on their teams. You're good at your job; you're just not in the right circle.

Why It Happens

Office cliques form—and thrive—for lots of reasons. Sometimes, for instance, you'll find bands of colleagues who have moved together from other companies, particularly in industries that are worlds unto themselves, such as media and technology. (And it makes sense: As leadership expert Herminia Ibarra points out, research consistently shows that the key to getting a new job is

FITTING IN: REBECCA'S STORY

WHAT HAPPENED:

I was thrilled when I got a foot-in-the-door position at a really hot company. But I was definitely low woman on the totem pole, with a low salary to match. On days that my coworkers rounded one another up for lunch, I literally couldn't afford to join them, but I wanted them to ask me. They were the office in crowd. Not only did they eat together—they shared weekend plans and tales, and had an easy, comfortable rapport with the boss. They were never mean to me, but I was invisible to them.

WHAT I DID:

I collaborated with one of the "cool kids" on a couple of projects, as her junior, and I worked really hard on them, which made her look good. She warmed up to me after that and started extending invitations to join the group for dinner and drinks after work—usually spontaneously, so I didn't have time to budget. But I said yes the first time I was asked, not wanting to lose my opening.

After that night, they still occasionally invited me along. And occasionally not. I didn't say yes every time—didn't have the cash—but I knew I'd somehow cracked the group. And with that, I was more accepted at work. I felt more part of things, and I think my work was better, too. I gained confidence. But in time, I also realized I more naturally gravitated toward people who took joy in their work. Bonding over drinks wasn't really my thing. So I started working, somewhat voluntarily, late nights in the office. Those of us who stayed after hours got free dinner and cabs home on the company, so money wasn't an issue. The dinners I shared huddled in an office conference room felt much more like bonding experiences to me. We talked about work, we talked about ourselves, we built mutual respect. Little by little, I found my own in crowd, and it was a much better fit.

DID REBECCA GET IT RIGHT?

Rebecca found a toehold into the clique, and that was all to the good, because it helped her integrate with her colleagues. And she learned soon enough that she was better off making personal connections with colleagues she respected and admired than hanging out with the flashiest group. Building her own in crowd worked beautifully, because those relationships would make her happier and more "connected" with her job in the long run.

networking.) When people know one another socially or from past jobs, they naturally have stronger, deeper ties.

Of course, they also tend to gel if they frequently work together on projects. They understand and trust one another's strengths and weaknesses, and even have shorthand ways of communicating that outsiders might not understand at first. In other words, they cultivate a group "emotional intelligence," to use psychologist Daniel Goleman's term. In teams, emotional intelligence can be critical to doing great work, but it's not automatic—it must develop over time.

When senior managers see a group operating so smoothly, why *wouldn't* they go with that well-oiled machine for the next big project? Though they don't mean to deny others chances to shine and advance, that's often the unfortunate outcome.

What to Do About It

If you find yourself outside the right clique at work, you may miss out on opportunities—both professional and social. But you don't have to sit at your desk just waiting for someone to notice you and invite you along. Break into the group—or build your own.

Work with the existing clique

Don't let the golden children get all the heat and light. Even if you're not invited to contribute to their big projects, express interest in them. Leadership consultant Ron Ashkenas advises, "You can say to your boss or colleagues, 'I know I'm not on that assignment, but could I sit in on a status meeting to learn more about it?'" And once you're in the room, offer to pitch in. Raise your hand for *any* role to start with, says Ashkenas: "Be willing to do some scut work to prove yourself." Volunteer for all-hands-on-deck QA work, for instance, or offer to update process documentation. When you do help out, overdeliver—and look for even more ways to showcase what you can do. People will start to see what you bring to the party, and in time you may find yourself a regular in the go-to group. Ashkenas recalls a client's secretary who successfully did this years ago. "She volunteered to sit in on meetings and take notes," Ashkenas says. "She created great summaries and eventually helped do some secondary research in support of the project. A few months later, my client had promoted her to an analyst role and hired a new secretary."

Another alternative, Ashkenas says, is to ask a member of the golden group to mentor you. That will require a long-term commitment on both sides. But if you can identify someone in the clique you could learn from—and she'd be willing to invest time and energy in your development—that might provide you with entrée as well.

Form your own alliances

Maybe chumminess at the office feels artificial to you or seems like a waste of time. You may be thinking, Why put aside my "real" work just to make friends? But the reality is, it'll help you do your work more effectively.

First, you'll gain support for your ideas. No matter how respected you might be individually, you'll always bolster your case by lining up allies. Suppose, for example, you're proposing a new CRM database. You'll need buy-in from your IT colleagues because they'll be involved in picking and maintaining the software if the project becomes a reality. So you'll want a buddy in IT to help you think through how to enlist his team's support before you bring your idea to senior managers.

Second, people will share more information with you if they feel connected to you. When they catch wind of a big decision or organizational change in the offing, *you'll* hear about it sooner—so you'll have more time to prepare for it. If you're not part of an informal alliance, people simply won't think to clue you in.

To form alliances that'll give your ideas traction and keep you informed, you'll need to network deliberately and efficiently. Ask your boss and a trusted mentor or two which people in the organization you should get to know better, suggest leadership consultants Kathryn Heath, Mary Davis Holt, and Jill Flynn. Set up lunches with those folks. Find out about their pet projects and challenges.

Flynn adds: "Get a big-picture view of whatever company you are working in. What are the challenges? Who are the leaders? Have that down cold in your mind." Then, she says, you can seize opportunities to talk with colleagues about these issues. But make your outreach subtle. "You shouldn't make an appointment to interview the person and just sit there taking notes," suggests Flynn. "Formal is your last resort."

Flynn coached someone who had identified a power player she wanted to learn from at her company. But he was busy and didn't know her well, and they didn't interact much on the job. So Flynn's client figured out a natural way to collaborate with him and build a relationship.

She offered to help him with a big training session he held once a year—to organize it, run errands, whatever he needed. He gratefully accepted, and that was the start of a productive mentoring relationship.

Create opportunities to socialize with the colleagues you're eager to know. Another client of Flynn's discovered that a couple of important people in her company took the train home at a certain time every day. So for a few weeks, she kept an eye out for them on their way to the train. When she spotted them, she walked along with them, chatting as they went. "It worked," Flynn says. "They became comfortable with her, and she learned a lot."

It's essential to do all this in a way that feels and looks authentic—you don't want to come off as a stalker. The key is to initiate relationships *before you need them,* so it's not just about angling for favors. Otherwise, you won't have the stomach for it, and you'll end up avoiding alliances rather than building them. And that can have a devastating impact on your career, says Kent Lineback, coauthor of *Being the Boss.* Very few people rise to the top of their profession without allies to support them along the way. It might be critical, for example, to have them backing your candidacy for a sought-after promotion. Or to have a go-to team for high-profile projects you need to knock out of the park.

Lineback knows this all too well. Years ago, he didn't focus on building relationships outside his own department, even though he held a senior management position. "I just didn't *want* to," he recalls. During a strategic-review meeting, Lineback shared his ideas about what direction the company should go. He was stunned when nobody responded with even a glimmer of enthusiasm. He had carefully worked through his proposal with members of his own group, but he hadn't gut-checked or socialized it with anyone in the room ahead of time. And no one there felt obliged to give him the benefit of the doubt—he didn't have anyone in his "camp." After the meeting, a consultant involved in the review pulled Lineback aside and offered his two cents on what went wrong: "You didn't build any bridges," he said.

"I knew he was right," Lineback says. "It was one of those instant recognitions. I hadn't wanted to dilute my idea, make it messy, by bringing other senior people in. Shame on me. After a while, you realize you have to be plugged in."

Connecting with colleagues doesn't have to be self-serving or manipulative. Be transparent with them about what you're hoping to achieve, whether it's gaining a broader understanding of the organization, exploring other career paths in the company, or something else entirely. But also make it clear that you want the relationships to go both ways. And then, of course, look for opportunities to support *them*.

This worked for Heath and Flynn, who formed an alliance back when they worked in different departments of the same company. Over the years, they've found ways to support each other, discovered opportunities for each other, and generally enjoyed working together. Initially Heath reported to Flynn, but they later became peers.

"It's not a social relationship," Heath explains, "but we're best friends in a professional sense." While they were trying to figure out how to navigate the company, they'd each pass along feedback or news that might be helpful to the other. "We would trade information," Heath says. On more than one occasion, they trusted each other to discuss job opportunities that would take them outside the company. "One time I was getting ready to take another job and she said, 'You're running away from something...'" Heath recalls. "We were pretty straight with each other. You need to have a truth teller in your group, and we just became that for each other."

They ultimately parlayed their successful partnership into a consulting firm, Flynn Heath Holt Leadership (with Mary Davis Holt). If you can build strong relationships with people you respect—as they did—the time you invest will have long-term benefits for you and your allies.

Chapter 9
The Credit Stealer

The Problem

You've put in long hours on a project, and some of your best ideas made the final cut. Yet no one knows it. When your colleague presented the final proposal at a recent team meeting, she didn't specifically claim all the credit for herself. But she avoided mentioning you and used the pronoun "I" every time she could. Afterward, your boss thanked her for doing such a great job—and your colleague still said nothing about your contributions. Once or twice this kind of thing could be an honest mistake. But it happens all the time. How will you ever get ahead if no one sees the good work you do?

Why It Happens

People may appear to take credit for your work without realizing it. When they're making a presentation or talking to a superior, they genuinely get caught up in their own role and simply miss the opportunity to name other key players. And collaborative environments can make it tricky to even identify who contributed what. Most bosses don't go digging for those details because what they ultimately care about is the team's work as a whole.

What's more, in some professions, the culture makes it very difficult to get credit for your work before you reach a certain level in the hierarchy. In management consulting, for example, the senior partner on an assignment usually gets the client's accolades, whether she's done the work or just supervised at arm's length. In academia, the tenured professor almost always appears first in an article byline, although her junior team may have done most of the research. Even in the court system, hardworking, bright judicial clerks help shape the opinions of their bosses without much—if any—recognition.

But sometimes, a more insidious motive lurks behind credit stealing: The thief is insecure or desperate to look better to her superiors—and figures she can get away with it if she's stealthy, says leadership and networking expert Brian Uzzi.

What to Do About It

Don't rush to point fingers. Consider whether there's any chance you're wrong. Maybe your colleague *did* have the same idea as you, or maybe you heard it kicked around somewhere else without remembering it. Uzzi's research suggests it's common for people to overvalue their own contributions. "It's called *fundamental attribution error*," he says. "We all think that our role is much bigger than everybody else's. Ask five people, 'How much did you contribute to this project?' Every person will say he did 50% of the work." So if you think someone hijacked the credit for your hard work, make sure your perception isn't skewed. "Check with others to see if they agree," Uzzi says. Don't just assume the worst.

But if, upon reflection, you *do* see a problem, try the following steps to solve it.

Stop it before it starts

If you've been burned before on a team, prevent it from happening again by writing down the group's expectations and assignments up front, advises leadership consultant Ron Ashkenas. Begin with a discussion about goals. Then, as a group, create a work plan that supports them: Lay out all the tasks, sequence them, and agree on individuals' assignments. If you and your colleagues draft the work plan together, there will be less room for confusion later about who was responsible for what. You'll also have a written history of your shared intentions. If your work involves a presentation, don't let someone fly solo. Divide up the slides—and share the visibility.

Clear the air

If you're not able to preempt the credit stealer, have a candid conversation with her. Give specific examples. For instance: "Sophia, when you presented our report, I was a little surprised when you said, '*I* stayed up all night...' because we both did. Can we talk about why you said that?" Many times just pointing out the behavior will put an end to it, says communication and branding expert Dorie Clark. Your colleague may immediately apologize and say, "I didn't realize it came across that way."

Or she may simply deny the charge: "That's ridiculous—I did almost all the work on this project myself." Don't accept that answer. Push back. Showing her that you won't quietly step aside makes it harder for her to gloss over your efforts next time.

Go to your boss

It's always best if you can work things out directly with your colleague. Tattling over a minor incident or two may antagonize her and put her on the defensive. "You don't want to create an enemy just because of a mistake," Clark advises. But after you've talked to her, if she refuses to see your side of the situation and continues her behavior, go to your boss. Otherwise, your morale and motivation will suffer. When you speak with your boss, keep your tone neutral. Talk about the impact on the business, not just on you, so that you won't sound petty or overly emotional. Maybe your colleague's grandstanding has caused others to avoid collaborating with her, for example, or your team is earning a reputation in the company for being embroiled and ineffective. Review the steps you've already taken. Suggest another solution or two that you've thought of, and ask your boss for his input.

What If the Credit Stealer Is Your Boss?

Many managers believe that a direct report's success is rightfully their success, too. After all, they laid out the vision, assigned the tasks, nurtured and developed the talent, and so on. In some organizations, Uzzi says, that's simply a given.

Your boss may not even remember where she gets every idea. And she may get annoyed if you seem easily wounded by what she considers a normal by-product of collaboration.

Take a long-term view

The "reward" for your contributions may not be immediate applause but something more tangible in the future—such as better resources for your group or a promotion down the line. That's how it works at MTV. A case study of the entertainment company found that many of its best ideas, such as the wildly popular *Real World* television series, actually come from unpaid interns. But as a policy, no single person or team gets credit. It's always "MTV" as a whole, largely because the company wants to retain intellectual property rights. But MTV does, Uzzi observes, track individuals' contributions. The people who make a significant impact during their tenure get the best recommendations for paid jobs at other companies looking for talent trained in the MTV brand.

MTV evaluates interns informally through observations of teamwork and feedback from peers. If someone consistently adds to the creative process or plays a significant role in developing a product that no one could have come up with alone—such as a new concept for a show—his contributions will get noticed. Comedian and nighttime talk-show host Jon Stewart used to be an MTV intern. He worked on a new idea called "being real," which became the DNA for reality TV and helped get Stewart on the short list of high potentials at MTV. MTV rewards team-based work by "basically being a big employment agency," Uzzi says, where placement in good, paying jobs after an MTV internship is the "currency used to reward people over the long run."

Even though your boss doesn't give you a nod for every accomplishment, your overall impact may not be lost on her. Does she have a track record of eventually rewarding those who've paid their dues? If so, it's probably worth being patient. If not, you may need to have a chat.

Tread very, very carefully

You can get credit without embarrassing your boss, but it's a delicate procedure. Organizational development and HR expert Susan Heathfield recalls a consulting client who did this effectively. Assigned to work on a companywide profit-improvement project, Heathfield's client ended up doing the lion's share of the research, but her boss delivered almost all the findings. That made sense because he needed to get buy-in for the ideas. But Heathfield's client wanted senior managers to know she'd played a key role. So she found ways to graciously add supporting facts and background information during meetings. She didn't upstage her boss, but she subtly demonstrated her level of knowledge and involvement with the project. "Over time," Heathfield says, "it became clear to the big bosses who really knew what was going on." The company promoted her to oversee the project full-time—"with huge kudos and credit," Heathfield adds.

Of course, diplomacy is critical. Don't try to put your boss in her place in front of others. "If she takes credit for your work, there's a very good chance she's doing it out of some deep-seated personal need for recognition," says Kent Lineback, coauthor of *Being the Boss*. So she won't forgive you for a public shaming—and she'll probably retaliate. Instead, advises Lineback, talk to your boss privately. Tell her that you're motivated by recognition for your ideas. If she doesn't start sharing the credit after you've brought it up, she's not likely to change her ways. Unless you can derive longer-term rewards from your work (as in the MTV example described earlier), it might be time to look for another job.

THWARTING THE THIEF: BERNARDO'S STORY

WHAT HAPPENED:
A colleague put one of my PowerPoint slides into his own deck—without mentioning my name in a source line. He just presented my ideas as his own.

WHAT I DID:
I went to see him and said, "I feel like this is my intellectual property. If you're going to use it, I'd like credit." But he pushed back, saying that people in our organization shared everything, so there wasn't a need for a source line. We went back and forth. When he still didn't budge, I involved third parties in our network—people we both respected. He knew if his reputation for withholding credit spread, no one would want to collaborate with him. So he backed down. Not only did he stop using the slide—he stopped giving the lecture entirely. All to avoid putting a single line of credit in a 40-slide deck. To him, giving credit diminished his originality in front of his audience. But in the end, he cut himself off from the very material that could have made him appear more original—and more collaborative.

DID BERNARDO GET IT RIGHT?
Bernardo handled the situation well. He approached his colleague respectfully and asked for nothing more than a source line—hardly an unreasonable request, even in an organization that "shared everything." Had he backed down, his colleague would have taken that as tacit permission to keep plagiarizing.

Chapter 10
Managing a Disgruntled Former Peer

The Problem

A recent, and well-deserved, promotion changed the social structure in your group. A pal and former peer now reports to you—and he doesn't like it. He acts as if he doesn't realize you're the boss, bypassing you whenever possible. Sometimes he's downright hostile. It's awkward for both of you. You're afraid you'll look ineffectual if you don't get it under control quickly, but you're not sure it's possible to fix the situation and save the relationship.

Why It Happens

It's common for a former peer to resist a reporting change like this. The problem stems largely from the complex issue of self-esteem, says Carol Walker, a principal at Prepared to Lead. We all benchmark ourselves against colleagues to gauge how much we've achieved, for instance, and how much people respect us. We don't even realize we're doing it most of the time. But when our guideposts change—as they do when a peer becomes the boss—it disturbs our sense of self, Walker points out. No one likes to lose relative position.

So your promotion probably dealt a significant blow to your peer's ego: He wasn't chosen for the role, after all. And he may have less access to senior leaders than before. If your promotion created a new level of management, for example, he may now be a rung lower on the org chart, reporting to someone with a lesser title. These are very real losses—and he might act out as a result. It can be especially difficult—on both sides—if he's older than you. You may feel guilty about the promotion and hyperaware of your youth; he may be embarrassed that he was passed over for someone less seasoned. That tension makes any interaction uncomfortable at first. And if you were friends, it complicates matters even further. You may struggle to maintain personal ties as you try to establish the parameters of your new professional relationship.

What to Do About It

It's tempting to dismiss your employee's reaction as shallow, selfish, or status-driven. You may even resent it, Walker says, and vent to others about it. Ironically, he's probably venting about *your* behavior, which may be less than sterling if your self-esteem feels threatened, too.

When your former peer doesn't respect the new pecking order, it can be difficult to empathize with him. But resist the urge to act out peevishly, Walker cautions. That would amount to stamping your feet in a childish tantrum and screaming "I'm the boss now—you have to do what I say!" As a manager—especially a newly promoted one—you need to make sure your people perform well. You'll get more energy and better contributions from them by fostering healthy egos.

So what should you do when your former peer lashes out? "Recognize the behavior for what it is—a natural reaction to unwelcome change," Walker says. "Your challenge is to restore equilibrium as quickly as possible."

Reset your own expectations

After a shake-up in the org chart, can you and your former peer still grab drinks after work? Can you continue to trade snarky comments about annoying colleagues?

Yes and no, says leadership consultant Jessica Pryce-Jones. You have to acknowledge that your relationship has fundamentally changed, even if you're good friends. You can't remain an inner-circle confidante—or treat your direct report as one—now that you're the boss. But that doesn't mean that you suddenly have to defriend your pal on Facebook or scratch his name off your holiday card list. Just put a little distance between the two of you. Find a new sounding board, and encourage him to do the same.

Expect him to test you to see how much of the original friendship remains intact. Maybe he'll ask you for information that you shouldn't share, for instance, or wait until you really push before he responds to your requests. You may be tempted to cave because you feel uncomfortable about the change in chain of command. But you have to set new boundaries. If your colleague asks you an inappropriate question—"How much are you budgeting for raises this year?" or "What does the CEO think of so-and-so?" or "What happened in the executive committee meeting this morning?"—don't answer. Count to 10 before responding, if you have to. Think about whether your boss would want you to share those details, and edit yourself accordingly. You can end the conversation with a statement such as "It's not appropriate for me to say right now." If you dismiss the question quickly but firmly, he will probably stop asking. If he persists, be direct: "You know I can't share confidential management information with you. Please don't keep asking me. I promise I'll fill you in when the time is right."

Check your perspective

Before going into problem-solving mode, though, make sure there's actually a problem to solve. You might be projecting negative feelings onto your new report ("I would feel that way, so that's how he must feel").

Step back and do a reality check, advises Pryce-Jones. Do you have concrete evidence that he's upset about the situation? For example, is he avoiding you? Meeting with your boss on his own without informing you? Has anyone told you that he's specifically complained about you? If not, you may be imagining hostility that doesn't exist.

Talk it out

If you do find evidence of bitterness, say something right away. Ideally, though, you'd ward off resentment as soon as you're promoted. In the beginning, it may be enough to show a little sensitivity and say, "I know we'll need to work through a new professional relationship. I hope we can be candid with each other about that." Delaying the conversation won't make it easier—it will only allow hard feelings to build up. Though you may be uncomfortable explicitly discussing the change in roles, you're in charge now, so it's your responsibility to take the lead.

It's not possible to have a comprehensive and constructive conversation about your new relationship the minute your promotion is announced. But briefly acknowledging that things are different now will help soothe frayed nerves and put you in a stronger position to have a positive, forward-looking conversation down the road. Assure your former peer that he's still one of your most trusted colleagues, and give him time to adjust to the new dynamic. And then, if he struggles with the transition, get that out in the open.

That's the advice leadership consultant Ron Ashkenas recently gave a client who'd been promoted to CEO over a tight-knit group of peers. One colleague in particular struggled with the new hierarchy because she'd wanted the job. Making matters worse, everybody who worked with them closely watched the tense relationship, viewing it as the new CEO's first test. "I advised him to have a private, honest conversation with his former peer," says Ashkenas. "That's how you defuse this

LEAPFROGGING: MICHAEL'S STORY

WHAT HAPPENED:

When I was in my late 20s, my boss created a new position for me that had me leapfrogging over two colleagues who used to be higher than I was on the org chart. They would now report to me. I was thrilled about the promotion, but I was so unprepared for it that I didn't pause to think through how to handle the situation with my colleagues. My boss told them he was promoting me and then briefly let me know that it hadn't gone too well, but that was my first and last conversation with him about it. One of them quit the next day. I felt terrible about it—I had considered us friends and didn't even have a chance to discuss it with him. But the other one, he stuck around. And that was worse than leaving, because he fought back with classic passive-aggressive behavior. We were in the middle of a huge project, and he suddenly went from putting in a great effort to doing the minimum. I kept finding mistakes in his part of the project and started panicking that he was actually putting them there on purpose.

WHAT I DID:

I did two very stupid things: First, I apologized to him for getting my promotion. And then I just worked harder. Instead of addressing any of the real issues, I decided that I personally had to make sure everything was perfect. It was exhausting, both emotionally and physically. He seemed to take pleasure in the frantic circles I was running. When the project was finished, I saw a mistake in the final report the first day it went public. I wanted to cry. When my colleague quit about a month later, I was relieved.

WHAT SHOULD MICHAEL HAVE DONE?

Michael didn't do anything right here. He was so unprepared to be the boss that he never *acted* like the boss. He didn't clear the air with his colleagues, so they had no choice but to assume (correctly) that he hadn't considered the situation from their point of view. When the first one resigned, Michael should have responded to the wake-up call by having an open, direct conversation with the remaining colleague. But by keeping mum and picking up all the slack himself, he just made it easy for that colleague to misbehave. From the beginning, Michael should have emphasized his desire for a productive relationship, clearly laid out the team's needs, and asked his direct reports how he might help them succeed in their roles.

kind of problem: You address it head-on and focus on both parties' needs. Say that you want to be successful in your role—and you want your new report to be successful, too." Ashkenas says that helped repair the relationship and alleviate tension so that the former colleagues could work together productively.

If you think the dynamics are strained, say so when you sit down to talk, suggests Pryce-Jones ("This isn't easy for either of us..."). Assure your colleague that you'll consider previous conversations confidential, especially if you've shared personal thoughts with each other in the past. Then talk about how you look forward to strengthening your working relationship. You're striking a balance here: Clarify what you expect from the other person—but also express your loyalty and support.

Even after you've taken these steps, does your former peer seem reluctant to open up? Offer a few observations about what you think his concerns might be, and then ask him to fill in the picture for you. Make it easier to discuss taboo topics such as visibility and status by bringing them up yourself. Tell him how much you value him and that you're committed to helping him reach his professional goals. Say you realize it'll take a little time to earn his trust in your new role. And ask him to speak up (respectfully) when you make mistakes so that you can learn from them. That will emphasize the two-way nature of your relationship.

Todd, a newly promoted manager in a small media company, recounts facing just this situation with his former peer Carlos. They had both reported to the same senior manager, but that person decided to have Carlos report to Todd instead. While the move was initially awkward for both of them, they went to an off-site lunch to hash out their concerns. When Carlos confessed to never feeling valued by the former senior manager in the first place, it was easy for Todd to build on their existing relationship of trust. "You know that I understand your strengths as well as anybody here," he said. "Tell me what you'd like to see yourself doing that you aren't doing already."

Of course, one air-clearing conversation isn't enough, says Ashkenas. You'll continue to face issues that require candid discussion. For the CEO in Ashkenas's example, meetings presented a challenge. When he raised provocative questions to stimulate healthy debate, his former peer froze, unsure whether it was permissible to challenge her boss in public. Puzzled by her silence, the CEO asked about it later in a one-on-one, and the colleague spoke openly about her concerns. That was the only way to identify and solve the problem: The CEO explained that he saw debate as a good thing, as long as it was collegial, and that thawed the ice.

Correct course

Even if you and your employee have both behaved badly and are feeling a little hostile toward each other, you can turn things around. Leadership and networking expert Brian Uzzi suggests the following three steps, based on his extensive research and consulting work in leadership and organizational change:

1. **Redirection:** Look for ways to redirect your new report's—and your own—negative feelings. For

instance, when you talk, try blaming circumstances rather than people. Set up the meeting in a conference room or an off-site spot. Calling him into your office would only reinforce that you are now in charge and he isn't. "Moreover," Uzzi says, "it shows you need to lean on the crutch of your authority. Neutral ground indicates that you have confidence in your leadership position." You might even try to find something *better* than neutral ground, Uzzi suggests, such as a place your new report likes. Meeting at his or her favorite restaurant can signal your intention to invest in the new report. "That can evoke positive feelings that spill over into the discussion," Uzzi says. As obvious as those tactics might seem, Uzzi's research shows that they *do* work. Redirection allows the person to continue feeling his natural emotions but shifts them from a destructive place to a safer one.

2. **Reciprocity:** Now that you're the boss, you'll need your new direct report to do things for you—preferably willingly. Before you ask for something, try giving him something: an unexpected perk, perhaps, or an opportunity to showcase a strength. Also, find common ground to discuss. Maybe you're both committed to the success of an R&D effort, and you share the view that the demographic of your ideal customer is shifting. Focus on addressing that—working toward a common goal will help replace the hostility with some-

thing more productive. You might, for example, ask him to attend an important management meeting so that he can inform the discussion with his technical expertise. By doing this, you'll signal that you're looking for ways for him to grow and gain exposure to more senior managers. You'll also demonstrate that you trust him to make smart contributions. Small steps like this will help lay a more positive foundation for your relationship. "The secret to effective relationship building through reciprocity is to give before you ask," Uzzi says. "If you give and ask at the same time, you don't create a relationship—you create a transaction."

3. **Rationality:** Have a rational discussion to clarify your expectations. You can't avoid this conversation; it's critical if he is to trust that your other steps (redirection and reciprocity) aren't just ploys to marginalize him by pushing him into new assignments or areas that might be out of the mainstream workflow. "To avoid skepticism creeping back into the relationship," Uzzi says, "never leave the conversation with the other party saying to himself, 'So and so was great to me in the meeting. He offered me many valuable things, but he didn't say what he wanted in return. I wonder when the other shoe will drop?'" Say what you need to, and be specific, whether it's "I need you to be my ally" or "We need to make some changes to your job description." Discussing

your expectations may actually relieve stress for your new direct report. A clear sense of what you expect of him, how he fits into the big picture, and what role he'll play for the team will allay his fears about you as the new boss. And, Uzzi advises, "Don't say you need the other person in a needy way. A good approach is to let the other party know that he or she is valuable and that your offer is distinctive, but that you also have other relationship options. This elevates the offer by expressing its value (others want it, too)." One way to do that, Uzzi suggests, is to say "I wanted to give you the right of first refusal..."

Bring your boss into the loop

Don't just hope *your* boss won't notice any adjustment problems you and your direct report are having, advises Walker. Let her know it's been a tough transition and explain how you're approaching the situation. She may have anticipated difficulties on both sides but held off to see if you could figure out a path on your own first, to show she does consider you to be in charge now. But asking her for guidance won't make you look "green" in your new role. View it as a chance to highlight your problem-solving abilities. Describe your game plan, but let her know you'd appreciate her feedback and other suggestions. Complaining about your employee's behavior without detailing what you're doing to manage it will only lead your boss to think that you aren't taking ownership. If she offers help, don't be afraid to accept. Is your former peer continually doing end runs around you? Ask your boss to redirect him back to you when he tries to go over your head with a problem. But keep your tone even and calm: Present yourself as sensitive, patient, and on top of the situation. Raising and addressing issues in a prompt and professional manner will help your boss see your management skill.

What if your colleague still acts up after you've tried all these tips? Then it's time to wield your new legitimate authority, says Stewart Tubbs, former dean of the College of Business at Eastern Michigan University.

"I had this situation myself with a couple of people who had wanted to be dean but didn't get the job," says Tubbs. "Boy, they were not about to cooperate with me when I was appointed instead. Eventually, I had to sit them down and say 'We can do this the easy way or the hard way. The easy way is I'll support you, you'll support me, and we'll work together. The hard way? If you don't come around, we'll have to start making things formal. We'll have 30-, 60-, and 90-day performance reviews. If you continue to rebel and aren't meeting your goals, I will take up the matter with HR in formal disciplinary proceedings. All things considered, I'd like to do it the easy way.'" Eventually, both colleagues left the university, having never really come around. But Tubbs felt that he had done all he could to get the relationships back in line before resorting to dramatic measures.

Of course, you can say all this in your way—in your own voice. But if you've tried everything else to no avail, you'll probably need to pull rank to put an end to the game playing.

Section 3
Political Challenges in Your Organization

Chapter 11
Surviving the Office Outing

The Problem

Your company has a couple of splashy employee events every year—and that kind of "forced fun" is not your cup of tea. You like most of your colleagues, but you dread the thought of trust falls, or pelting one another with paint balls, or laughing politely at your boss's bad jokes over charred burgers and potato salad. You'd rather skip it, but everyone is expected to attend, so your absence would be duly noted.

Why It Happens

Companies organize events like these with good intentions—often to raise morale, help employees blow off steam in an informal setting, foster team building and idea sharing, or reward people for good performance. After all, research shows time and again that engaged employees are far more likely to be loyal to an organization, and those with friends in the workplace are both happier and more productive. But the challenge is knowing exactly how to socialize with coworkers you're *not* already close to: Whom do you talk to? What if the conversation doesn't come naturally? How can you make a good impression without feeling fake? How do you strike the right tone? How much should you let your guard down? Where do you draw the line between casual and inappropriate? These sorts of questions can stress you out and prevent you from enjoying the very benefits the event is meant to provide.

What to Do About It

You have to make a reasonable effort to participate. It's not uncommon for people to bow out, citing pressing deadlines or last-minute conflicts—and many companies don't make social events mandatory. But as communication and branding expert Dorie Clark points out, avoiding them sends a bad signal. It suggests you're disinterested in the company and your colleagues—or perhaps that you don't see a future for yourself there. Those perceptions aside, the carefully crafted excuse you make once might be greeted with skeptical smirks when you use it a second or third time.

Here are some guidelines for gracefully navigating office outings and actually getting something positive from them.

Find a comfortable way to participate

If you're lucky, you welcome the opportunity to hang out with your coworkers because you're fond of them. But even if that's not the case, says leadership coach Susan Alvey, a principal at Pemberton Coaching, assume the most positive perspective you can. "Instead of looking for the first moment to escape, think about how you can have a good time." If the outing involves something you can't imagine yourself doing, you don't have to go *all* in. You'll get extra credit with your colleagues, Clark adds, just by showing a little team spirit. If you really can't stand to play "ultimate Frisbee," for example, get involved in a different way. Go and cheer on your teammates. Bring lemonade to the barbecue afterward. Take photos. But show up.

Focus on connecting

View the outing as a personal-growth exercise, Clark advises: "Use it to hone one of the most talked about, but least practiced, skills in corporate life: asking questions that draw people out and then really *listening* to their answers." Before your event, think about what you could ask your colleagues—even boring Floyd from HQ—that would help you relate to them. "It's a low-stakes laboratory," Clark says. If you can figure out how to engage with Floyd, you can also learn to have richer conversations with clients or collaborators.

Beth Weissenberger, an executive coach, agrees: "I ask my clients before they go to an event, 'How many people will you meet?'" Give yourself a concrete, obtainable goal. For example, you might plan to have conversations with five colleagues you don't know well—or make a point of speaking to the CEO for the first time.

Part of connecting is letting more people know who *you* are. This doesn't mean you need to chat up everyone in your path or prattle on about your accomplishments. "When people are nervous, they either retreat or talk incessantly about themselves," observes Boston University's Kathy Kram. A better way to make your presence felt is to demonstrate your sincere interest in others. "As you encounter people," she says, "really focus on building the relationship. Express genuine curiosity instead of worrying about being impressive. Listen, and then share your thoughts in response to what you're hearing." And if you're shy, don't torture yourself to overperform. "It's not necessary to stay to the bitter end," advises Kram. Just meet your goal and gracefully excuse yourself. You don't have to make a big deal of leaving—try a simple "I've enjoyed talking with you. I'm going to head out now, but I look forward to learning more about your project next time I see you." No one is taking attendance at the end of the party. A trip to the bathroom could take a discreet left turn to the coatroom and out the door.

Don't check your inhibitions at the door

Of course, as you're trying to relax and be yourself, you'll want to maintain some sense of decorum. We're all adults—and most of us know our limits—yet we've all seen people have too many drinks at office events. Yes, an extra glass of wine might ease your frazzled nerves or help you endure sitting next to the world's most pedantic colleague, but be more disciplined with your intake than you would with close friends. People aren't likely to notice what you're drinking, but they'll certainly notice if you start acting goofy or making indiscreet comments. And they'll remember serious missteps for a long time.

If you mess up, own up

So what if you wake up the morning after and realize that you may have crossed the line at the office party? "If you do something embarrassing, own up to it," Alvey says. You don't need to send out a mass e-mail to everyone in the company. But have the courage to apologize to anyone who witnessed your behavior.

If it happened in front of a group, touch base with each person individually. Don't belabor it—self-flagellation isn't required. Alvey recommends a short, direct statement along these lines: "I realize that my behavior might have put you in a difficult position, and I never meant to do that." Or try a little bit of humor, company culture permitting: "No more punch for me!"

Admit the mistake, apologize, and move on. "Psychologically, it might seem easier to slink around and try to avoid people," Clark says, "but ultimately, that's not the right thing." *You* become the elephant in the room. People might whisper when you walk in, or you'll catch them staring at you or laughing. It may or may not be about you, but your imagination will run wild. Much better to put the elephant away by taking control of the apology. That way, at least, smirks, eye rolls, or looks of pity can't catch you off guard. You'll have already owned up.

Make amends face-to-face if you can. But if you feel that e-mail is your best option (perhaps because it's the only way you can manage to get the words out), omit the embarrassing particulars—written messages stick around and may be forwarded.

If your mistake was a big one, apologies might not be enough. Weissenberger recently worked with a media company that fired a new employee in his first week because he got drunk at an event and ended up making out with a subordinate.

"Once you mess up your reputation, it's hard to get it back," Weissenberger says. "Not impossible, but hard."

Chapter 12
Lasting Through Layoffs

The Problem

Something big is happening in the senior ranks at your company, and it can't be good. You've noticed lots of closed-door meetings and heard rumors of layoffs. Everyone you know feels vulnerable. You've seen colleagues chatting up muckety-mucks and taking them out to lunch, but that feels calculated and phony to you. You want to keep your job—and ideally take on more responsibility if there's an opportunity—but not by glad-handing the leadership team. How can you protect your career without sacrificing your self-respect?

Why It Happens

Even strong companies go through reorgs, for a host of reasons: CEOs face constant pressure to do more with less. New leaders want to put their mark on the firms they run. Organizations rework their business models to stay competitive in evolving industries. When times are changing, even the most stable, reliable departments can be seen as obstacles to progress.

As much as we'd like our leaders to include us in any thinking about pending layoffs, they have to keep the information closely held. It's probably painful for them to have those closed-door meetings—they know they're about to make life-altering decisions. But the last thing they need is for panic to set in while they're sorting out the specifics. There's still work to be done. A company can't lose its day-to-day momentum. And legal and security considerations may make it impossible to share information more widely—the organization can't risk having employees take valuable data, contacts, or intellectual property out of the building when they get wind they're going to lose their jobs. When layoffs do come, the news must be announced on a very tight schedule to control who knows what, and when, no matter how much compassion a well-intended manager may want to show his employees.

What to Do About It

When forces beyond your control threaten to reshape your organization, don't just passively await your fate. Create a survival strategy. You'll have a far better chance of sticking around and maybe even improving your position. This isn't about playing games or backstabbing others—it's about managing how decision makers perceive you and the value you bring.

Keep calm and carry on

It's easy to imagine all kinds of things happening behind those closed doors. But you might be wrong. Or maybe you're right to suspect a reorg, but there's still plenty of time for names to change on a layoff list. Either way, it does no good to fly into a panic. Act like a survivor, not a victim. That's what *Harvard Business Review* authors Janet Banks and Diane Coutu say in "How to Protect Your Job in a Recession" (September 2008), and it's good advice no matter what the economic climate. You don't have to be stoic or turn into a corporate cheerleader. But maintain your composure and professional demeanor—demonstrate your ability to focus and keep up your good work, despite swirling uncertainty. If you stop going full throttle because you might be out the door tomorrow, you're not doing yourself any favors: You may land yourself a spot on the layoff list if one does exist.

So rise above whatever back-channel chatter may be consuming your colleagues, says leadership consultant Jessica Pryce-Jones. People who spend a lot of time whispering aren't proving themselves indispensable. It's natural that the topic of pending layoffs will come up, especially when the boss is out of earshot. And there's always someone in the group who excels at sniffing out gossip and wants to share tidbits. But don't indulge in those discussions—walk away from the coffee machine if the conversation devolves. Quickly get meetings back on track when people start griping instead of working. Be a leader, even if you aren't officially one.

If you need to talk through your fears, turn to a trusted friend or relative. "Don't air your concerns with colleagues or in a way that your boss might hear," cautions one manager who has led teams through corporate restructurings several times in her career. That goes double for venting on Facebook or Twitter: It can only harm your chances of surviving if colleagues or managers see you as a complainer or, worse, a confidentiality risk.

That said, you'll need to keep up your network connections in a time of job uncertainty, says communication and branding expert Dorie Clark—and social media will help you do that. She notes that LinkedIn activity can signal when layoffs are brewing: You'll suddenly see lots of people in an organization updating their profiles and adding new connections. Get ahead of the LinkedIn rush, advises Clark. Refreshing your profile early on will allow your contacts to receive your skills and experience updates before hasty detail changes and requests to connect come through en masse from panicked peers. You can also start putting out feelers for informational interviews and job leads by touching base with former colleagues and superconnectors in your network. Often when people are laid off, they're given just a few minutes to clean out their desks—and they're not allowed to take any information, including contacts, from their computers. So make sure your LinkedIn connections are current and active long before you get called to HR for an unscheduled meeting. Also, tweet about industry trends you're noticing, smart articles you're reading—anything to show your contacts that you're still engaged in your work.

Mentally prepare

If you're bracing yourself for layoffs, much of your stress comes from losing control. Big decisions that will affect your future are out of your hands. Though you probably can't prevent a reorg if one is in the works, you can get ready to weather one—which will help alleviate some of your anxiety.

Start by visualizing scenarios: What will you do if you lose your job? How about if you keep your job, but you end up on a team of one, doing work that was previously handled by six people? And so on. Develop a Plan B, C, and D, with strategies ranging from seeking a new position in the company to signing up with different headhunters to taking a sabbatical to consider what you'd like to do next. In practical terms, it's always wise to keep your résumé up to date. But if you haven't done that, give it a fresh look and see if you can jazz it up with new experiences, skills, and responsibilities.

Also, assess your rainy day fund—how long can you afford to be out of work? (Clearly, it's not the best time to make a down payment on a new house or sign a lease that requires stretching your salary.) If you don't have much of a cushion to fall back on, map out your expenses and see where you can start saving. All this helps you reclaim some control, which puts you in a more constructive frame of mind. You'll be less inclined to engage in politically risky behavior, such as kvetching with colleagues, making bitter remarks to your manager, or openly surfing the internet and looking for jobs instead of doing your work.

And try to get a sense of how long the reorg process will take, says Pryce-Jones, so that you'll know how far you'll have to stretch your resilience. If you have a good relationship with your boss, ask about the time frame for pending decisions, or discreetly tap your broader internal network for clues.

Get ahead of your boss's questions

Downsizing is often about streamlining operations. In large-scale restructurings, for example, companies typically focus on producing more and spending less, not on cutting specific individuals loose. With this in mind, Pryce-Jones advises, try to suss out your boss's concerns—and help address them.

If you feel comfortable approaching your boss directly, do so, and present yourself as a problem solver. She might not be at liberty to let you in on specifics, but she may still welcome a proactive conversation. You could open with something like, "I realize you probably can't share details at this point, but I'm guessing you've had to consider how we might do things more efficiently. If you'd like, I can share some ideas in a brief proposal. Am I jumping the gun, or would that be helpful?" Tell her you've been thinking through how the team can shave time off a complicated process, for example, or handle more tasks. Arm her with solutions to recommend to decision makers.

Position yourself

Don't assume your manager and others above her already know how valuable you are. Show them, says leadership coach Susan Alvey. Write up your contributions to the company, and sit down with your boss to review them—even if the potential for layoffs isn't out in the open. Your boss will certainly figure out that you've picked up the vibe, but there's no reason to wait to put your best foot forward, as long as you don't appear desperate or pushy. You're indicating that you know she has difficult decisions to make and you want to make your best case to stay. Give her an updated résumé or just a list of bullets. But clearly spell out how you've added to the organization's success. This makes it easy for her to forward your document or copy and paste from it as she formulates her plan. If she's agonizing over which names to put on a layoff list, she may be grateful for reasons to keep you aboard.

Of course, don't suggest other candidates for that list. Your boss probably knows where the dead wood is, and your pointing it out will signal that you aren't a team player. This also isn't the time to say how underappreciated you are or how much a layoff would hurt you ("I'm the primary breadwinner in our family"). That's the last thing she wants to hear if she's struggling with a tough layoff decision—and it can actually make you more vulnerable by giving you a pathetic aura. Rather, Alvey says, emphasize the positive: Remind your boss of projects and accomplishments that demonstrate your breadth and depth of skill and your ability to adapt.

Your goal is to make a strong case for why you deserve a spot on the new, streamlined team. Quantify the value you add to the company, suggests Clark. If, for example, you bring in revenue that offsets big costs, pull together a simple spreadsheet that highlights this. If it's hard to

103

calculate your impact in dollars—perhaps you're a communications specialist, for example—find ways that you *can* keep score. Track the number of media hits you get for your company and how much your company's Twitter following has increased since you've been leading its social media efforts. Do you work in an operational role? Document productivity improvements you've made. You don't have to cite *every* achievement. Hit the highlights,

---

REINVENTION: HANNAH'S STORY

WHAT HAPPENED:

Where I work, a major restructuring brought two previously battling divisions together. My boss and the other unit head became comanagers of the combined group, so neither division "won" over the other. But as they began to articulate a vision for the newly formed unit, I could see that my role would soon become outdated.

WHAT I DID:

I polished up my résumé, highlighting skills that I knew would be useful in the new structure, and shared it with my managers. And I asked lots of questions about changes to our strategy and business model to show that I cared about where we were headed as a group. Essentially, I reintroduced myself to my managers and proposed changing my role to better support their evolving goals. I was genuinely enthused about the possibilities I'd identified, which I think showed.

DID HANNAH GET IT RIGHT?

By clarifying what her role could become—and showing that she had the skills and experience to pull it off—Hannah secured a place for herself and for several of her direct reports in the new order. Though she didn't know for sure whether she'd have a job after the dust settled, she acted in a way that said "I'm with you," which signaled strength, flexibility, and loyalty. She figured out how she and her team could help her managers implement their strategic plans instead of waiting for them to sort everything out.

and be ready to continue or deepen the discussion if your boss requests it.

Still feeling uneasy after reviewing your skills and contributions with your boss? You may want to discuss alternatives to layoffs. Say you've learned that your organization is cutting a certain amount from its budget. Would you volunteer to go half-time to keep your job? Could you suggest job sharing? "It's a risky strategy," Alvey says, because you might give something up without needing to. But you may be able to have an honest conversation in the abstract: "Would it make a difference if some people went part-time?" Talk about possibilities without necessarily offering yourself up as a sacrificial lamb. If you enlist your peers to have similar conversations with your boss, the team effort might succeed without costing individuals too much. But if your colleagues get scared and back off, you could find yourself the only one with a thinner wallet.

Engage at a higher level

Pryce-Jones urges her coaching clients to learn everything possible about the company's new direction or strategy. Be curious. Ask good questions: Why has the strategy changed? What were the driving forces? And keep up with news about your industry. If you understand the larger context in which your company is operating, you'll better equip yourself to survive changes. "Be as proactive as you can as soon as you can," suggests leadership consultant Ron Ashkenas. "The more you can be part of the discussion, the more you can influence it." Talking with your boss has already given you some perspective, but find out what pressures other departments face. Speak with other unit heads and peers with internal influence. It's entirely possible that your boss won't have any say in the specifics of the layoffs at all—higher-ups are making those decisions. So it's critical to make yourself known, in a positive way. The more perspectives you gather, the better informed you'll be. And if people can see that you're a curious, intelligent participant in conversations about the company's future, you'll increase your chances of being part of it.

About the Author

Karen Dillon is a coauthor of *How Will You Measure Your Life?* (with Clayton M. Christensen and James Allworth). She was the editor of *Harvard Business Review* from 2010 to 2011 and is now a contributing editor. A graduate of Cornell University and Northwestern University's Medill School of Journalism, Dillon began managing people very early in her career, which led to a particular interest in the topics of leadership, developing talent, and managing yourself. Ashoka, a global network of social entrepreneurs, named her one of the world's most influential and inspiring women in 2011. Follow her on Twitter: @DillonHBR.

Smart advice and inspiration from a source you trust.

Whether you need help tackling today's most urgent work challenge or shaping your organization's strategy for the future, *Harvard Business Review* has got you covered.

HBR Guides Series

HOW-TO ESSENTIALS FROM LEADING EXPERTS

HBR Guide to Better Business Writing
HBR Guide to Finance Basics for Managers
HBR Guide to Getting the Right Work Done
HBR Guide to Managing Up and Across
HBR Guide to Persuasive Presentations
HBR Guide to Project Management

HBR's 10 Must Reads Series

IF YOU READ NOTHING ELSE, READ THESE DEFINITIVE ARTICLES FROM HARVARD BUSINESS REVIEW

HBR's 10 Must Reads on Change Management
HBR's 10 Must Reads on Leadership
HBR's 10 Must Reads on Managing People
HBR's 10 Must Reads on Managing Yourself
HBR's 10 Must Reads on Strategy
HBR's 10 Must Reads: The Essentials

Buy for your team, clients, or event.
Visit our site for quantity discount rates.

hbr.org/books/direct-and-bulk-sales